Bioclimatic Skyscrapers

Ken Yeang
Bioclimatic Skyscrapers

With essays by Alan Balfour
and Ivor Richards

Artemis   London   Zürich   Munich

First published 1994 by
Artemis London Limited
55 Charlotte Road
London
EC2A 3QT
England

British Library Cataloguing in Publication Data
A CIP catalogue entry for this book is available
from the British Library

ISBN 1 874056 56 0 (London)
ISBN 3 7608 8424 5 (Zürich)

Designed by Borja Goyarrola
Printed in Hong Kong

Contents

Architecture for a New Nation   7
by Alan Balfour

The Tropical High-Rise   9
by Ivor Rchards

Theory and Practice   16
by Ken Yeang

Design Principles   28

Buildings and Projects   33

Appendix: Climate and Design   139

Acknowledgements   144

Architecture for a New Nation

Professor Alan Balfour

Two distinct and related qualities are present in the architecture of Ken Yeang. The first is the ingenious and aggressive body language of the work as it struggles to reconcile the discontinuity between architectural form and climate. This anthropomorphism is consistent within the recent suite of towers; they seem like armoured figures preparing for an as-yet-undefined task, somewhat uneasy with their ecological responsibility. The second, more potent but elusive, can be found in the way the work achieves a definition and a presence of a new culture.

In searching for an effective means of framing this second quality I was reminded of the young Eero Saarinen who was entering architecture with the emergence of the Finnish nation. Saarinen set himself the task of conceiving its future in architecture. He travelled across Europe experiencing the most potent work of the avant-garde, returning to Finland to construct a building embodying what he felt was the poetic promise of the new nation. He was informing his imagination to will through architecture a brilliant new reality, a vision that continued to grow as Europe struggled to recover from the First World War. It was finally realized in the creation of a vast ethereal tower, a man-made mountain, that was to inspire a nation. The nation, however, was the USA, not Finland, and the symbolic content was to enhance the reputation not of a people but a newspaper, the Chicago Tribune.

An intriguing aspect of this comparison with Yeang is Saarinen's ability to give form to the dreams of one culture that released hidden desires in others.

The evolution of Yeang's architecture is embedded in the emergence of Malaysia as a distinct culture. One hundred years and more of imposed and quite alien reality would make the task of establishing the cultural voice of Malaysia after British rule more complex than freeing Finnish culture from the dominance of Russia. South-east Asia has experienced various forms of European influence since the 16th century. The British established a permanent colony on the Malay Peninsula in 1826 that was not to be disturbed until the Second

World War, after which continuing political instability led to British withdrawal in 1957. The Federation of Malaysia was formed in 1963. Ken Yeang was at school in England in the early 1960s and joined the School of Architecture at the Architectural Association in London in 1966, when its teaching offered the most compelling visions of the future, the technological fantasies of such figures as Cedric Price and the Archigram group. From the AA he went on to Cambridge and more specialized work in the sciences and the environment, and from there to the landscape programme at Penn with Ian McHarg. These were the raw ingredients he took back to Kuala Lumpur – the heady visions of the AA, the determinism of Penn, and the environmental morality of Penn.

The spirit of Archigram even in Yeang's recent work is neither a chance nor a casual presence, for Yeang continues to maintain strong links with London. All these influences are still present in the work and the imagination, yet a transmutation has occurred in the desire to form a response to the nature of a Malay and Asian reality through the forces of climate. His analysis of the traditional housing of Kuala Lumpur, written in the last decade, and his distinguished history of Malaysian architecture, published in 1993, are the clearest evidence that the form and content of Yeang's work must be measured within the broader context of cultural politics.

The restoration of a regional and national identity after a century of British rule had specific targets: how to negate the presence of the British past; how to inflect architecture with modernist reason while detaching it from Europe's tendency for symbolic abstraction; how to frame an architectural language which, while showing an understanding of traditional values, would express the economic ambitions of the new nation. His towers as they ascend in Kuala Lumpur or Penang or Ho Chi Minh City seem, in their paradoxical mix of orders and desires, to achieve a synthesis exactly appropriate to the cultural promise of South-east Asia, their warrior-like stance ready for the economic revolutions of the new century.

The Tropical High-Rise

Professor Ivor Richards

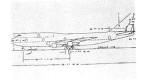

Ken Yeang's doctoral thesis on the development of a framework for looking at the built environment and its relations to the natural systems of the biosphere established the essential agenda for his life's work, dedicated to the development of an ecologically responsible architecture for the 21st century. During the last 15 years of practice a stream of projects, mainly high-rise buildings for the tropics, has steadily developed these principles. Events such as the Rio summit of 1992 and the 1993 UIA Congress in Chicago – both of which focused on issues of sustainability, energy and the conservation of the natural systems of the world and its interactive environments, habitats and their inhabitants – indicate that Yeang's work is now at the leading edge of contemporary architecture.

Awareness of these issues does not itself constitute a new ideology. In the 1960s, for example, Buckminster Fuller's work foreshadowed many of today's concerns. Fuller's projects included sea-farming on a scale that would ensure adequate food supplies for a developing world population.[1] Ideas like this go beyond even the concept of building – an approach shared by another seminal influence, Cedric Price, then teaching at the Architectural Association in London.

Price and the emergent Archigram figures were among the influences that Yeang experienced as a student, together with the famous Tropical Studies School. The work and beliefs of Richard Neutra and the concept of survival through design were also significant to students in the 1960s. These influences, and many other diverse sources – from designers like Victor Papenek[2] to economist-prophet Fritz Schumacher[3] – created an acute awareness of what the mission of a designer in the late 20th century might encompass, varying according to region, programme and local context.

Since the 1960s, the 'global village' itself has emerged as a growing reality. It is now possible to identify a range of architects who are developing an ecological architecture in different regions of the world, both temperate and tropical. Among them are, for example, Nicholas Grimshaw whose recent Seville Pavilion considered both sunpath and the use of the waterfall-wall;[4] Alsop and Störmer's Hôtel du Département in Marseilles, France, deals with the seasonal wind, the Mistral; the Richard Rogers Partnership's Tomigaya Tower project uses the wind to generate power. Foster Associates' Commerzbank tower in Frankfurt will incorporate large open-air atrium gardens and natural ventilation, interactive with both the atrium and the zoned exterior double-skin. Renzo Piano and his Building Workshop have had a long involvement with an ecological, evolutionary process that generates new buildings like new species in nature. Another parallel is the responsive, shielded forms that characterize the practice of Ralph Erskine in Sweden.

In recent history, Wright, Neutra and Schindler all exhibit the dual tendencies of response to region and climate, and the work itself – such as Wright's Solar Hemicycle – is shaped literally by these passive considerations. And again in the 1960s, the influence of Reyner Banham and his analysis of the 'well-tempered environment' was another aspect of a growing bioclimatic culture in architecture.[5]

Creative engineers play a vital role in the multi-disciplinary world of contemporary practice; the collaborative work of Renzo Piano with Peter Rice is an particularly outstanding example of structural and detailing innovation. In the field of environmental systems and integrated structure young partnerships such as Battle McCarthy or Max Fordham, both from the UK, exhibit a completely fresh attitude to systems and form, allowing their advice to grow naturally from principles.

Research and practice

The early years of Ken Yeang's practice saw the development of an attitude and a particular working method that achieved innovative results related to

climate-driven theory in projects for commercial clients. Today, other architects are beginning to share his concern for an ecological architecture that can be created within realistic, economic market conditions.

Underpinning Ken Yeang's work agenda is his personal methodology of Research Development and Design (RD+D). Implicit in this is his insistence on building his research and constantly improving his architectural production, a commitment that is rare amongst architects who have to achieve their commissions for a profit-driven clientèle. The results Yeang has achieved within this context are often commendable and his ability to hold a leading position within a field of international architects and patrons requires a sound basis both in management of ideas and in development.

In Ken Yeang's office the medium in which all his activity finds expression is the design process itself and the crucial structure provided by his own agenda for his research programme.

A summary of the Yeang agenda includes the following:

<u>Sunpath projects:</u> tropical high-rise buildings, mainly offices. The arrangements of the cores are determined by sunpath and the provision of buffer zones. Cores include natural ventilation for toilet modules and fire stairs. Orientation determines the position of glazed areas. Sun shading is incorporated and often associated with balconies, or skycourts, that create buffer zones and provide both shade and break-out from the interior, coupled with planting that is introduced over the entire elevation, often in spiral formation. This constitutes the architecture of the environmentally interactive wall.

<u>Wind rose projects:</u> these projects are also either for high-rise offices or for linear cluster apartment towers. The techniques used include opening up the plan into clusters allowing air movement related to prevailing winds and orientation. Innovations include the provision of wind-wing walls and skycourts, drawing air into the inner spaces for natural ventilation, and the experimental use of roof-level

aerofoils to assist air flow within the section incorporating the stack effect.

Menara Boustead in Kuala Lumpur City is the first of the truly green 'hairy' office towers whose plan-form also establishes the basis for the type. This was the direct precursor of the Menara Mesiniaga, the second tower by Yeang for IBM, the archetypical culmination of the sunpath projects. Situated on an open site, it is a landmark building signalling the future city on the route in from the airport. The form of the building is powerfully effected by the skycourts and the sun-shaded roof and its facilities, together with the separated cores that in their edge condition both shield the interior of the tower and are naturally ventilated. The glazed north and south walls are a response to the tropical overhead sunpath. The other strong formal element is the shaped, ramped landscape plinth housing entrance, computer suites and underground car-parking in sheltered basements.

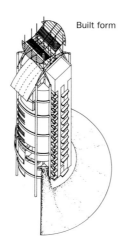

Built form

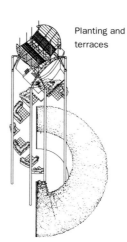

Planting and terraces

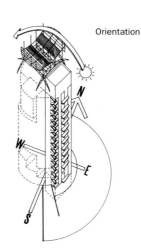

Orientation

Glazir
shadi

The wind-driven projects and other towers for sites in China are all work in transition. The projects are being wind-tunnel tested and final detailing is being done, but a general impression can be gained from the plans and models of the MBf Towers, which experiment with holes in

the façade for natural ventilation of interior circulation. A similar principle is used in the cluster form of the Penggirian apartment tower.

A recent competition for a 'EuroTower' in Glasgow, UK – a visitor centre and viewing facility – provoked a response from Yeang which is his most animated to date. The expressionist strength of this bioclimatic skyscraper also incorporates clearly defined principles for all climatic regions from cool to tropical – an adaptable, friendly, structural fantasy.

The future

For the next stages of his work, Yeang is looking at the possible uses of rainwater and water-spray walls that induce evaporative cooling. Conservation of sites with ground-level filter beds, reintroducing rain to the land form instead of wasting it to drainage systems, is also under review.

Beyond this lie two further research ambitions:

<u>Cladding and Skin:</u> materials research, taking account of life-cycle and time.

For instance, structure is seen as long-life while cladding is short-life, recyclable and subject to refit and remodel pressures. Both energy performance and image can be upgraded as materials develop and occupancy changes.

<u>Lifestyle patterns:</u> here Yeang's intentions extend into sociological projections. The basic thesis is very clear – that is, if you want a society to live within a framework of ecological principles, then lifestyle and its containers (buildings) must evolve and change together.

Yeang's first book focused on his ideas for the tropical city.[6] His current research goes further and relates back to the work in progress. Looking beyond the building itself, studies relate to the street, the city block and the overall urban arrangement, including transportation. Viewed as interactive energy systems, these factors take on a fresh significance – for instance, transportation is both a great consumer of energy and a major source of air pollution. It is clearly a crucial factor in the design of the city and hence Yeang has begun to incorporate this in his projects.

What is in evidence here is the activity of an architect who is systematically at work on the whole built environment. This is entirely consistent with his first proposals at Cambridge University in 1972, and the work has continued into practice ever since.

At the heart of the principles are the first and dominant concerns of energy reduction and buildings as open systems – interactive inside and outside in response to the seasons. In essence, the fundamental propositions are very simple, but the overall, global effect of their consequences represents an optimistic and progressive vanguard of potential that is crucial to the effort towards a sustainable future world.

Reviewing a specific range of projects, such as Menara Mesiniaga, the inevitable questions of the relation of the work to both the Malaysian Far East context and the state of modernism itself arise in parallel. The response in this case is both integrated and self evident. The architectural zeitgeist is expressed through technology and materials, state-of-the-art thought and attitude and the incorporation of climate and lifestyle principles as a contemporary translation of context.

Emotive references to traditional materials and forms are avoided, an attitude validated from a realistic position that proposes a Malaysian architecture for the 21st century, very different from its historical origins. This is an open attitude that can absorb change. It is also an intelligent reflection of a polyculture establishing a positive identity as a collective, through abstract contemporary form.

The external form and its contextual response is not dealt with as an issue of style and aesthetics in the traditional value sense. Rather, the modernist vocabulary is extended by the manipulation of light, elegant structure and adjustable loose-fit membranes and skins, with protective attachments. Integration with nature is a central issue. The overall arrangement abandons traditional geometry and responds to the dynamics of climate, sunpath, wind direction and the issue of lifestyle: openness – including breezeways, verandahways, transitional spaces that relate to the society they serve. The same attitude applies to the interior concept, with the interaction of interior and exterior spaces, light and air as aspects of low-energy building, and open systems.

The building as a response to the physical and social environment is not a new idea. But, in the continuum of Ken Yeang's work, it beautifully compliments the smaller-scale equipment that goes to make up a contemporary lifestyle appropriate to an emergent world nation and its future needs for a sustainable environment, in harmony with the profuse natural world in which it is situated.

1 R Buckminster Fuller, 'What I am Trying to Do', catalogue of projects, RIBA (London circa 1967), with attendant lecture appearance.

2 Victor Papenek, Design for the Real World, 2nd revised ed., Thames & Hudson (London 1985).

3 Ernst Friedrich Schumacher, Small is Beautiful – a Study of Economics as if People Mattered, Abacus (London 1973).

4 See Structure Space and Skin: The Work of Nicholas Grimshaw and Partners, ed. Rowan Moore, Phaidon (London 1993).

5 P Reyner Banham, The Architecture of the Well-tempered Environment, 2nd ed., Architectural Press (London 1969).

6 Ken Yeang, The Tropical Verandah City, Longman (Kuala Lumpur 1987).

Theory and Practice

Ken Yeang

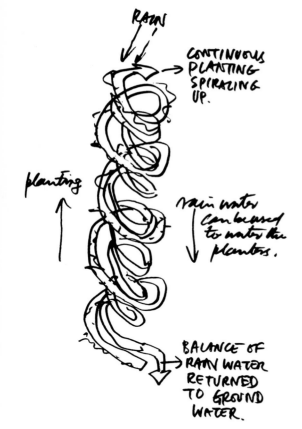

RAIN

CONTINUOUS PLANTING SPIRALING UP.

planting

rain water can be used to water the planters.

BALANCE OF RAIN WATER RETURNED TO GROUND WATER.

Crucial to our entire agenda and work is the focused methodology of research, design and development (RD+D). This involves an approach to the craft and practice of architecture that demands research as the basis for design and, further, insists on physical implementation as the testing ground for ideas and their poetic interpretation.

Over the last 15 years, our RD+D work on tall buildings and towers has led to a new building type, the bioclimatic skyscraper. Theoretical propositions provide an alternative to the ubiquitous cookie-cutter-floorplate prismatic tall building now found throughout the major cities of the world.

The first questions to be asked are: what is a tall building and is there a theory for the design of the tall building? But an even more niggling question is, can there be architectural theory at all? For architectural theory can be perceived as an admirable endeavour to make architecture theoretical rather than a body of theory that is architectural (cf M Linder, 'Architectural Theory is No Discipline', in J Whiteman, J Kipnis, R Burdett (eds), Strategies in Architectural Thinking, MIT Press, 1992). Being theoretical involves the architect borrowing the techniques and disciplines of the scientist or the philosopher. While this may be grand in describing a particular architect's œuvre, or beneficial in propping up an architect's work or approach to design, it ignores the fact that architecture does not share many features with philosophy or science.

In practice, architectural design is a craft, and a variable one at that. Post-modernism has successfully shown up the volatile nature of this craft by its unrestrained use of architectural symbolisms, its frivolous multiplication of the surface area of the built envelope, its prodigious use of unnecessary building materials, its indifference to engineering economy, its extravagant use of land, and its irrational subservience to whim and history instead of the allocation and restriction of excessive consumption of energy resources.

Looking at the global economy today, one has to be increasingly aware of energy as a scarce resource; the need for architects to design for a sustainable future becomes a self-evident imperative. Here lies a likely trump card for affirming theoretical respectability: the design of energy-efficient enclosures has the potential to transform architectural design from being an uncertain, seemingly whimsical craft, into a confident science. The theory for the design of the tall building might then be one that derives from energy conservation.

However, this energy equation in design is only part of a greater gestalt in environmental design. Regarded independently, there are essentially three routes to low energy consumption in architecture: through material and component selection, through supplier economics (i.e. a life-cycle approach from 'source' to 'sink'), or through basic design. It is the last route that provides the starting bases for much of the design work here and for the explanation of the buildings' configurations.

My earlier research work (at the University of Cambridge, 1971–1975) had been on the formulation of an environmentally comprehensive framework for looking at the built environment and its relations to the natural systems of the biosphere. A simple partitioned matrix was used to provide a compact structure for describing the sets of inter-relationships and inter-actions that a built system has with its environment (cf F E Emery and E C Trist, 'The Causal Textures of Organisational Elements', in F E Emery (ed), Systems Thinking, Penguin Books, 1969). This matrix also reveals some new meanings in these relationships that can be helpful for design.

Our current research and development work on the bioclimatic approach is essentially a sub-set of broader environmentally responsive design strategies. We find that there are basically two justifications for the bioclimatic approach, one a comfort-based rationale and the other a passive, low-energy one. The latter eventually was found to be expeditious for us in explaining our environmentally responsive design agenda to commercially minded clients. Energy savings could be easily accounted for in terms of monetary savings.

Absence of design criteria

Although bioclimatic principles are relatively well advanced for low- and medium-rise buildings, there has yet to be adequate attention and research directed at tall buildings. Justifications for greater attention are obvious. Traditional building types cannot suffice as design models for the high-rise since the scale and bulk of the high-rise far exceed any precedent. The tall building being largely a novel (i.e. non-traditional) building type, with new servicing systems, it requires its own set of design premises even though the fundamental principles of designing with climate remain unchanged.

Historically, tall buildings were structures that symbolized religious or imperial power. However, in contemporary times the high-rise, while continuing to exhibit physical dominance, has replaced this religious or imperially expressive role with that of the commercial commodity. We might compare the high-rise building to the Boeing 747 in that, like the airplane, it has become an international piece of technology which every national economy possesses. Even some of the poorest countries in the world have their own fleet of 747s and a number of high-rises in their urban areas. The question then becomes: how do we personalize and make use of this international machinery in a way that enables it to be related to its geographical context?

It might be argued that attention should be given to the wider contextual aspects of bioclimatic urban design or planning. However, most countries do not have the financial capacity to prepare a tabula rasa and start anew with relocated urban centres of low- or medium-rise buildings. Furthermore, if the present urban centres were to be replaced, discarding existing extensive infrastructure investment would be wasteful of resources.

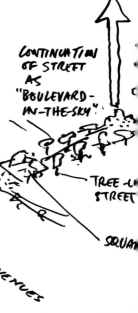

Besides this, the pressures of increased land values, urban accessibility, expanding urban populations, globalization of commerce and the locational preferences of businesses make tall buildings inevitable. What should be of concern therefore is the way these are designed and whether there are effective planning controls on their location, urban design and built-form height.

Architects faced with having to build intensive developments in dense urban contexts require design criteria for this building type. Besides the Chicago/New York models, we find that not even the largest of our traditional or colonial buildings (where these exist) can provide models for the new tall building.

Directed research in this field is needed. The fast pace of urban development, particularly in the Asia-Pacific region, makes the case for having adequate models for designing the environmentally responsive high-rise even more pressing.

The tall building typology

The skyscraper is essentially a multi-storey building generally constructed using a structural frame, provided with high-speed elevators and combining extraordinary height with ordinary room spaces such as would be found in low buildings.

Geometrically, the skyscraper can be regarded primarily as an intensification of built space over a small site area (or over a small built footprint). The tall building type permits more useable floor-space to go higher, to make more cash from the land, put more goods, more people and more rents in one place. The high-rise might be seen as a wealth-creating mechanism operating in an urban economy; it derives from high land values and these are related to urban accessibility, which is in turn a product of road and rail services. The environmental justification is that the high-rise's concentration of commercial activities in an urbanized location enables the reduction of energy consumption in transportation.

IEW TO RIVER

ACES / SKYCOURTS
EQUIVALENTS TO
SQUARES

The building becomes an
exterior of the
city's boulevards,
extend upwards.

The tall building is also the culmination of a number of building inventions: the structural frame and wind-bracing, new methods of making foundations, high-speed elevators, air-conditioning, flush toilets, large pieces of glazing and window framing, advanced electronics and telecommunications, sophisticated indoor lighting, ventilation and cleaning technologies.

In aggregate, skyscrapers are creations that result from the optimization of land costs and building economics, the locational preferences of their occupants, the desire for flagship status of their owners induced by the assertive image associated with the high-rise, and ingenious feats and inventions of architectural and engineering design. However, in optimizing the land-area use, tall buildings seek to have the maximum internal area on each floor (net areas) and the maximum gross building area for the site (i.e. maximum plot ratios and minimum net-to-gross ratios). In order to achieve these economic objectives, the following criteria became critical:

- minimum external wall thickness
- minimum vertical support size
- minimum horizontal support thickness
- minimum vertical circulation/service core area
- minimum floor-to-floor height.

The cost justifications for these are obvious. Minimum external wall thickness, reduced vertical support sizes (i.e. column sizes) and efficient core areas increase the net useable (rentable or saleable) floor areas per typical floor. The minimum horizontal support thickness and floor-to-floor heights lower structural costs and the area of external cladding and hence construction costs.

These are optimizing criteria for design based on efficiency and economy. They do not provide any theoretical construct for design. These criteria, if taken to their conclusion (whether in the case of the low-rise or the high-rise building), will lead to instances where building economics are given precedent over the aesthetic, human or poetic aspects of architectural design. In this case, the built form that results inevitably ends up as a diagrammatic, bland, inarticulate and geometrically efficient box. If there is to be a theory of tall-building design, it has to extend beyond building economics.

The bioclimatic rationale

What is the justification for designing with climate? Designing the tall building to take advantage of the meteorological data of the location inevitably means some physical and economic departure from the criteria outlined above. For instance, sun shading increases the thickness of the external wall; external lift cores may be less efficient than a central-core layout. What justification might we have for this departure, besides, of course, reasons of architectural aesthetics?

The most obvious justification must be the lowering of costs as a result of decreasing energy consumption in the operation of the building. This can be by as much as 40 per cent of the overall life-cycle energy costs of the building since the bulk of energy consumption happens during its operational phase. Significant savings in operational costs would justify incorporation of climatically responsive design features despite higher initial capital construction costs.

Another rationale derives from the impact on the users of tall buildings. The climatically responsive tall building can enhance its users' sense of well-being while enabling them to be aware of and to experience the external climate of the place. Research in the UK and Japan has shown that more than 40 per cent of users of tall buildings would like the option of being able to open windows to the outside. A climatically responsive design should provide the building's users with the opportunity to experience the external environment (and diurnal and seasonal changes) and, in doing so, to avert the blandness of spending their working hours over a significant part of the day in an otherwise artificial environment that remains constant throughout the year.

A further justification is ecological. Designing with

climate would result in a reduction of the overall energy consumption of the building by the use of passive (non-mechanical) structural devices. Savings in operational costs derive from less use of electrical energy which is usually derived from the burning of non-renewable fossil fuels. The lowering of energy consumption would further reduce overall emission of waste heat, thereby cutting the overall heat-island effect on the locality.

There is a further justification – a regionalist one. Climate, viewed in the overall perspective of human history and built settlements, is the single most constant factor in our landscape, apart from its basic geological structure. While socio-economic and political conditions may change almost unrecognizably over a period of, say, one hundred years, as may visual taste and aesthetic sensibility, climate remains more or less unchanged in its cyclical course. History shows us that, with accumulated human experience and imagination, the architecture of the shelter evolved into diverse solutions to meet the challenges of widely varying climates, indicating that the ancients recognized regional climatic adaptation as an essential principle of architecture. In this regard, the climatically responsive building can be seen as having a closer fit with its geographical context.

However, bioclimatic factors should not be the only design determinants. There are others such as views, site constraints, etc. Furthermore, if adopted over-rigorously, the designed solution may again appear like a diagram. Therefore, these aspects and principles should remain as guides for interpretation rather than as dogma for form. The bioclimatic energy-conserving agenda provides us with a set of theoretical principles for shaping buildings which must eventually allow for a permissiveness in poetic interpretation by design.

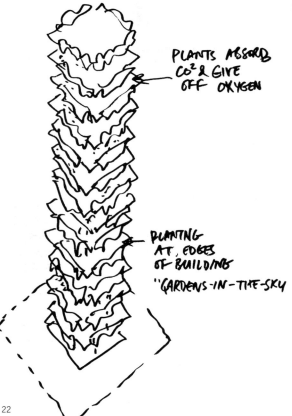

PLANTS ABSORB CO² & GIVE OFF OXYGEN

PLANTING AT EDGES OF BUILDING "GARDENS-IN-THE-SKY"

TRELLIS WALL

Future agenda

Our future agenda will obviously involve more on-going research, design and development work into other bioclimatic aspects as well as other ecological influences on building design: the beneficial use of wind and rain, the life-cycle approach to the use of materials and building equipment, and the development of new patterns of internal life for the users of tall buildings. The last involves seeking new patterns of spatial configurations that depart from providing building users with an environment that is simply a concrete tray in the air.

The design agenda

Our earlier projects (1984–1993) focus on a number of biological and ambient environmental factors for design. These include a preoccupation with the integration of vegetation with buildings (IBM Plaza; Menara Boustead; Menara Mesiniaga; Tokyo-Nara Tower), the opportunities for the placement and incorporation of transitional spaces in the high-rise built form (Plaza Atrium; Menara Boustead; Menara Mesiniaga; BP Tower); and the influence of sun on the built form and its external wall design (Menara Budaya; Central Plaza; Orchid Tower). Current projects explore the use of ambient wind both as a free energy source and as providing opportunities for design features (Penggiran Apartments; China Towers).

As described above, initial research and development had focused primarily on developing a broad theoretical base for the ecological design and planning of the built environment (1971–1974). The practice that followed (T R Hamzah & Yeang Sdn Bhd, from 1976) began with the problem of how to integrate and better relate vegetation with buildings. The starting premise is that vegetation is an important indigenous aspect of place and should therefore be an important regionalist design factor, besides being ecologically vital. It might also be argued that vegetation (and other biotic components of the location) needs to be introduced into the built

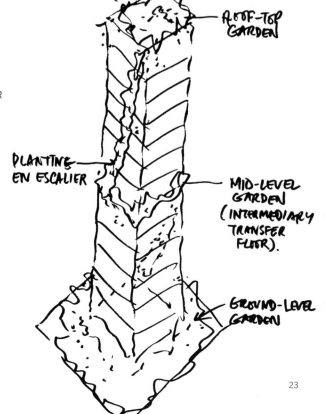

ROOF-TOP GARDEN

PLANTING EN ESCALIER

MID-LEVEL GARDEN (INTERMEDIARY TRANSFER FLOOR).

GROUND-LEVEL GARDEN

ZIG-ZAG PLANTING

environment in far greater abundance than is currently common. The built environment is rapidly covering the biosphere's entire surface with impermeable and virtually inert tarmac and paved or roofed surfaces.

Buildings might be regarded as being simply massive concentrations of inorganic mass extracted and produced all over the biosphere, piled up and assembled at a single location. The result is a significant increase in inorganic mass placed at that point. This needs to be balanced by an equally significant increase in planting and vegetation compatible with the location. The beneficial overall effect is not only the reduction of the likely heat-island effect for the locality; it will also make use of the oxygen-producing properties of planting to create an air-cleansing local environment in addition to absorbing much of the carbon dioxide and carbon monoxide emitted by the concentration of built systems.

The problem of the abiotic/biotic synthetically designed relationship between planting and building might be described as essentially one of designing the relationship between the built systems which are primarily inorganic (as in reinforced concrete construction, in steel or masonry, etc.) and the organic materials (plants, soil, etc.).

Theoretically there are three ways to relate buildings and planting: by juxtaposition, where one material is placed next to the other, as in the use of planter boxes (for example, Menara Boustead); by intermixing, as in the combining or interspersing of large areas and quantities of vegetation with inorganic areas or surfaces (for example, the mound of Menara Mesiniaga; IBM Plaza), and finally, by integration. Essentially integration is the ideal condition where there is a seamless intermeshing of inorganic and organic material (partially achieved in the Lake Club Competition Project in 1985).

Future work might focus on the greater use of organic and biodegradable building materials to increase the integration of planting and vegetation with the built system, greater use of trellises on walls for planting, the

ROTATING
SHIELD
(SOLAR & WIND)

use of porous external walls as planting bases, and the use of organic building materials for greater integration.

Our second area of preoccupation is with the creation of variable deep air zones at the façades of buildings, either as transitional spaces, or as interstitial spaces, or as residual spaces. These can be in the form of large open-to-the sky naturally ventilated atriums with overhead louvered-coverings (for example, Plaza Atrium), or recessed balconies (for example, Menara Boustead), or large skycourts (for example, Menara Mesiniaga).

These transitional spaces are partially successful in creating a layered building façade. They also soften the impact of the flat and hard faces of the built system on its external environment and provide semi-enclosed and in-between shaded areas at the upper parts of the building. Most users wish to have openable windows to permit fresh air to enter into the space and to enable more direct contact with the outside environment. However, the provision of openable windows (as in Menara Boustead; Menara Mesiniaga; China Towers) might be further extended by providing occupants of tall buildings with the ability to go out into an in-between space such as a terrace or balcony located at the upper parts of the tall building.

While it might be argued that in many cities, noise, smells and pollution would totally negate the benefits of skycourts and balconies, it might equally be argued that the aesthetic benefits to users and the simple provision of choice overwhelmingly surpass the factors militating against their provision. Furthermore, not all faces of the building will encounter street noises, noxious smells or aerial pollution.

Skycourts further provide opportunities for users to add planting, to personalize the landscaping as gardens-in-the-sky. They also provide commercially useful interstitial spaces for future expansion (for example, in the event of future increases in plot ratio enabling a larger structure to be built).

By providing courtyards in the sky, the tall building

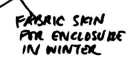

ING

FABRIC SKIN
FOR ENCLOSURE
IN WINTER

becomes more that just a stack of concrete trays for its occupants. They now have a greater level of choice in determining their personal environment. Full-height sliding glass doors opening onto the skycourts not only enable a better quality of daylight to penetrate the internal spaces, they also act as valves permitting wind to enter the building in the event of power failure or whenever natural ventilation is needed (without air-conditioning).

A fundamental aspect of architectural design must be the creation of new forms of internal life for a building's users. The provision of skycourts gives options for occupants in their use of spaces in the sky. Furthermore, in temperate climatic zones, skycourts provide occupants with opportunities to experience directly the changing seasons of the year. In this way the quality of life of the building's occupants is enhanced.

In tropical climatic zones, transitional spaces are already evident in much traditional architecture (for example, as verandahways and terraces); these spaces are a crucial part of the local lifestyle at ground level. Incorporation of skycourts in tall buildings enables us to recreate existing ground-level conditions in the spaces in the sky.

Explorations into the layering of the external wall from the inside to the outside environment, interfaced through transitional spaces, led to our concern for a variable external wall design. There followed a series of studies on the external wall as a varied skin that changes its sectional profile depending on its solar orientation (e.g. Menara Boustead; Menara Budaya; Orchid Plaza).

In certain conditions, this external wall might also be designed to be environmentally interactive, with parts that move, adjust and adapt depending on the external seasonal changes and local meteorology. The wall position might also change depending on the occupants' internal space use and demands (for example, Menara Mesiniaga; Autumnland Tower).

Current work involves exploration of ambient wind as a design influence and feature. Wind-gust velocities at the

upper parts of tall buildings can be significant (nearly 50 metres per second in downtown Kuala Lumpur). The proposition here is that this ambient wind energy might be incorporated as free energy in the building's design to increase the cross-ventilation opportunities to the inner parts of the tall building. This energy might also be stored to power some of the building's M&E systems (for example, in China Tower 1). However besides the self-evident ecological benefits of this proposition, this environmental factor could also provide new opportunities for sculpting design features.

In the layout of the typical floor (for example, in Penggiran Apartments, Blocks A and B), each apartment can be designed as an individual unit in the sky. Each can be detached from the others with minimal or no party walls (metaphorically similar to a detached bungalow). Each apartment unit becomes accessible from the common lift-lobby and the escape staircases by linked bridges and sky-walkways. In the typical floor layout, each apartment might have external walls all round it, increasing cross-ventilation as well as providing opportunities for cooling heat-gain arising from insolation.

Wind-related explorations include incorporating at the wind-leeward façades of each apartment unit some protruding devices (wing walls) that collect the wind and channel it through floor ducts and side walls to ventilate the inner parts of each apartment or space.

Following the wind-related design explorations, future work will continue with research on other climatic factors affecting building design both sculpturally and systemically. These include studies in rain and ground-water. Macro aspects of research and development may focus on the bioclimatic and ecological aspects of town planning and urban design, on material and equipment selection and their life-cycle considerations by the designer before installation or fixing.

Studies will eventually be directed towards life-style changes arising from these and other aspects of low-environmental-impact design.

Design Principles

Service core position is of central importance in the design of the tall building. The service core not only has structural ramifications, it also affects the thermal performance of the building and its views, and it determines which parts of the peripheral walls will become openings and which parts will comprise external walls. Core positions can be classified into three types: central core, double core and single-sided core. In the tropics, cores should preferably be located on the hot east and west sides of the building. A double core has many benefits. With both cores on the hot sides, they provide buffer zones, insulating internal spaces. Studies have shown that minimum air-conditioning loads result from using the double-core configuration in which the window openings run north and south, and the cores are placed on the east and west sides. The same considerations apply in temperate zones.

Lift lobbies, stairways and toilets should be given natural ventilation and a view out where possible. Inevitably, this means that they should be on the periphery of the useable floor space. External periphery placement of these parts of the building results in energy savings since they will not require mechanical ventilation and they demand reduced artificial lighting, as well as eliminating the need for additional mechanical pressurisation ducts for fire protection. Aesthetically, by placing these service zones on the periphery, they receive sunlight and have views out which are not possible with a central-core position. The user of the building leaving an elevator at an upper floor can see out and be aware of the place, instead of entering an artificially lit lobby that could be anywhere in the world.

Tall buildings are exposed to the full impact of external temperatures and radiant heat. Accordingly, the overall building orientation has an important bearing on energy conservation. In general, arranging the building with its main and broader openings facing north and south gives the greatest advantages in reducing insolation (and the resulting air-conditioning load). It frequently happens that

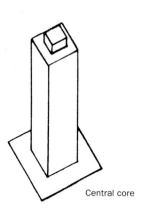

Central core

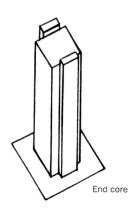

End core

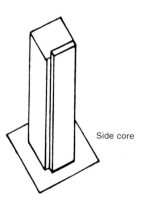

Side core

Cores at hot side

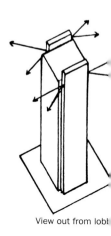

View out from lobb

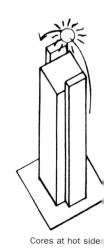

Site/building
adjustments

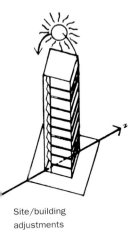

Site/building
adjustments

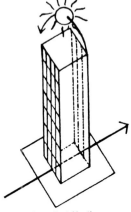

Curtain wall at North
and South faces

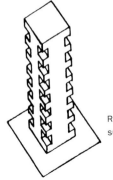

Recessed
sun-spaces

the geometry of the site does not coincide with sunpath geometry. In these cases, the other built elements may, if expedient for planning purposes, follow the site geometry (for example, to optimize basement car-parking layouts). Typical floor window openings should generally face the direction of least insolation (north and south in the tropics). Corner-shading adjustments or shaping may need to be done for sites further north or south of the tropics or for non-conformity of the building plan to the solar path.

Generally, window openings should orientate north and south unless important views require other orientations. If required for aesthetic reasons, curtain walling may be used on non-solar-facing façades. On other faces of the building some form of solar shading is required, while the quality of light entering spaces should also be considered. In temperate zones, transitional spaces can have adjustable glazing at the other face so that balconies or recesses can act as 'sun spaces', collecting solar heat, like a greenhouse or conservatory.

Deep recesses may provide shade on the building's hot sides. A window can be totally recessed to form a balcony or a small skycourt that can serve a number of functions besides shading. Placing balconies on hot elevations permits glazing to these areas to be full-height clear panels. These can give access to the balcony spaces which can serve as evacuation spaces, as large terraces for planting and landscaping, and as flexible zones for the addition of future facilities.

Large multi-storey transitional spaces might be introduced in the central and peripheral parts of the building as air spaces and atriums. These serve as 'in-between' zones located between the interior and the exterior. They should function like the verandahways of the old shop-houses or the porches of early nineteenth-century masonry houses of the tropics. Atriums should not be totally enclosed but should be placed in this in-between space. Their tops could be shielded by a louvered roof to encourage wind-flow through the inner areas of the building. These may also be designed to

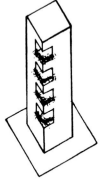

Site/building
solar skycourts

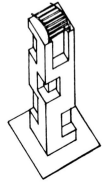

Transitional spaces

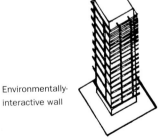

Environmentally-
interactive wall

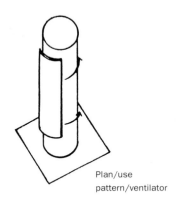

Plan/use
pattern/ventilator

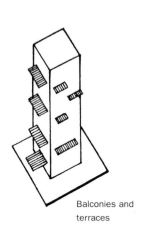

Balconies and
terraces

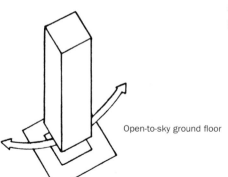

Open-to-sky ground floor

Vertical landsca

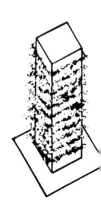

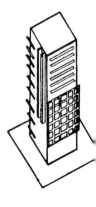

Shading devices

function as wind scoops to control natural ventilation to the inner parts of the building.

External walls should be regarded as permeable, environmentally interactive membranes with adjustable openings (rather than as a sealed skin). In temperate climates the external wall has to serve very cold winters and hot summers. In this case, the external wall should be filter-like, with variable parts that provide good insulation but are openable in warm periods. In the tropics the external wall should have moveable parts that control and enable good cross-ventilation for internal comfort, provide solar protection, regulate wind-driven rain, besides facilitating rapid discharge of heavy rainfall.

The building plan, in addition to responding to the commercial intentions of the building (for example, enabling single, double or multiple tenancies), should reflect the patterns of life and culture of the place, and its climate. In part this involves an understanding of the spatial modalities of the people, the way they work, the way culture arranges privacy and community. This can be reflected, for example, in the plan configuration, the building's depth, the position and layout of entrances and exits, the means of movement through and between spaces, the orientation and views as interpreted in the plan. The plan should also reflect air movement through the spaces and the provision of sunlight into the building.

Work spaces, even in a high-rise commercial development, have to have some degree of humanity, some degree of interest and some use of scale. For example, large skycourts and terraces might function as communal spaces as well as means of ventilation for the upper parts of the building.

The ground floor in the tropics should preferably be open to the outside and naturally ventilated. The relationship of the ground floor to the street is also important. The introduction of the indoor atrium at the ground floor may mean the demise of street life. Free-standing fortress-like buildings also tend to separate the building from the pavement, further alienating the street.

Free-standing buildings become isolated on their plots.

Planting and landscaping should be used not only for their ecological and aesthetic benefits, but also to cool buildings. Planting should be introduced as vertical landscaping to faces and inner courts of upper parts of tall buildings. Plants absorb carbon dioxide and generate oxygen, benefiting the building and its surroundings.

Solar shading is essential for all glazed walls facing the sun (generally east and west in the tropics). A number of configurations of passive devices can be used (fins, spandrels, egg-crates, etc.), depending on façade orientation. Shading blocks insolation in summer and prevents heat penetration of the building all year round in the tropics and in summer in temperate zones.

Cross-ventilation should be used (even in air-conditioned spaces, to cope with system breakdowns), letting fresh air in and exhausting hot room air. Good air movement promotes heat emission from the human body surface and gives a feeling of comfort. Skycourts, balconies, and atriums as open spaces and transitional spaces at the upper parts of the tall building encourage wind flow into internal spaces. Side vents operating as wind scoops located at the edges of the façade capture wind and make the best use of the high wind speeds found at upper levels. Wind can be channelled into ceiling plenums to ventilate inner spaces.

Good thermal insulation of the building skin reduces heat transfer, both from solar gain and loss of coolness from the inside. A second skin (a rain wall) can be built over the inner wall with an air gap in between.

Structural building mass may be used to store heat. The mass loses heat during the night and keeps internal spaces cool during the day. In temperate climates, structural and building mass can absorb solar heat during the day and release it at night.

A water-spray system on hot façades promotes evaporation and therefore cooling. In temperate climates, solar windows or a solar-collector wall can be located on the outer face of the building to collect the sun's heat.

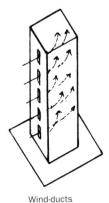
Wind-ducts

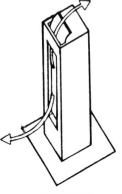
Wind-scoops

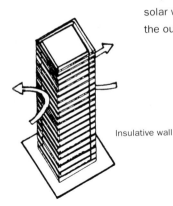
Insulative wall

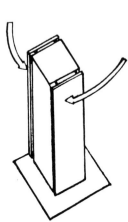
Structural mass

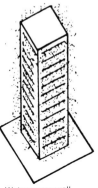
Water-spray wall

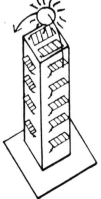
Solar-collector wall

Buildings & Projects
1981–1993

Camera Towers
1992–1993

Location
Sungei Besi, Kuala Lumpur,
Malaysia

Client
Selangor Turf Club

Size
12 m to 16 m high

1

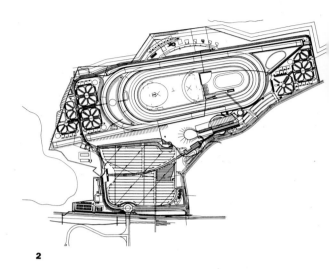

2

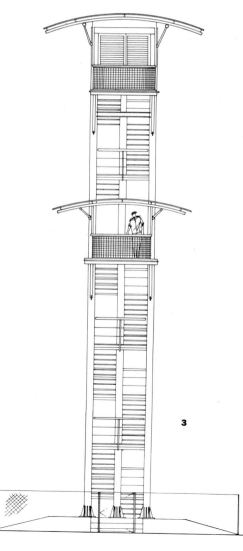

3

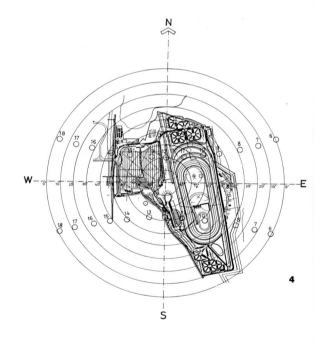

4

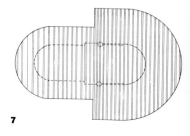

7

A series of camera towers located at various positions around a race-track. Their orientation is determined by the best viewing angles. The structure is a steel-frame tripod stiffened by the staircase as secondary framing. Sun shading and protection from rain is provided for the top platform on which race-recording video cameras are located. A canopy is also provided for the intermediary platform which used by the racecourse judges.

In the context of the development of bioclimatic towers, these can be seen as prototype structural armatures, with independent internal staircases, upon which habitable spaces and pods might be clipped.

5

6

1 View of tower
2 Site plan
3 Front elevation
4 Sunpath diagram
5 Side elevation
6 Detail showing stewards' platform
7 Roof plan
8 Plan: camera platform
9 Plan: steward observation platform
10 Ground-floor plan

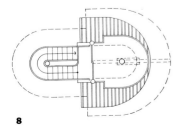

8

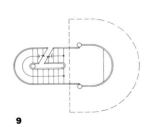

9

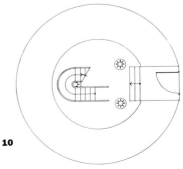

10

Ho Chi Minh City Tower
1992–1994 (target)

Location
Ho Chi Minh City, Vietnam

Client
Kinta Kelas

Size
19,684 m² gross
(14,286 m² net) with
1448 m² of car parking;
26 storeys

Plot ratio
1:10.4

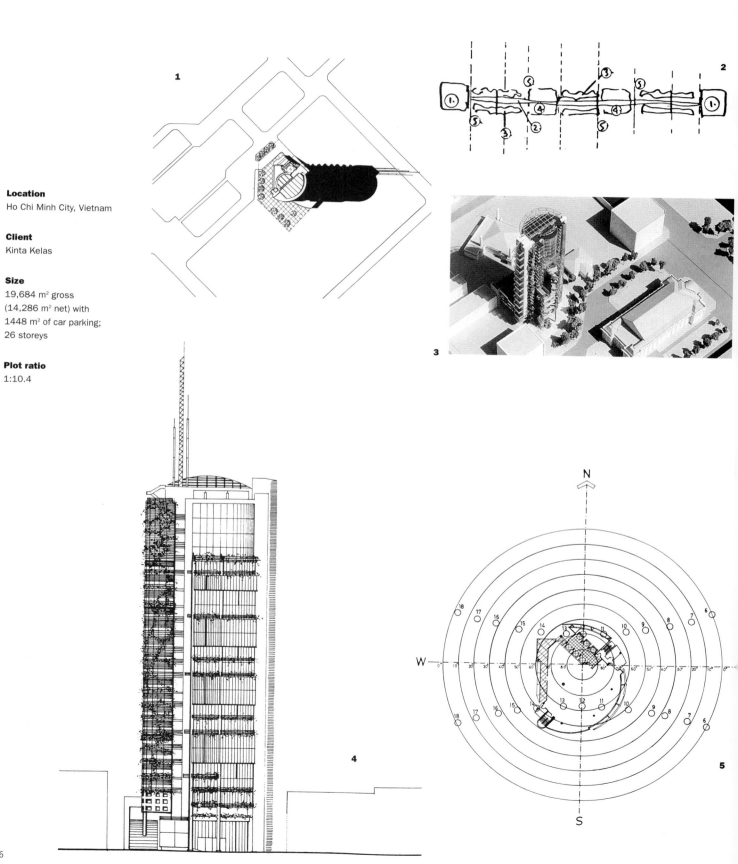

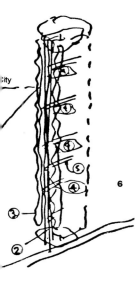

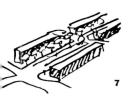

6

7

The programme called for a landmark commercial building for sale and rental. In response, the design concept is that of a 'boulevard in the sky'. Located at the end of a boulevard in this French-influenced colonial city, the tower emulates its tree-lined avenues through skycourts, trellis planting surrounding the glass lifts, and a planted penthouse. The lift lobbies, stairways and toilets are low-energy spaces, being naturally ventilated and lit; bridges off the lift lobbies give access to the skycourts. The west sides of the building have terraces and sun-shading, reducing the air-conditioning load. Terraces have sliding glass doors that control the natural ventilation of the office spaces (when regular air-conditioning is switched off during brown-outs).

9

1 Site plan
2 The city boulevard, showing tree-lined sides, squares, intersections and beginning and end focal points
3 Urban context model
4 Elevation
5 Sunpath diagram
6 The boulevard in the sky
7 Sketch of the city boulevard
8 Bird's-eye view of model
9 View of model from north-west

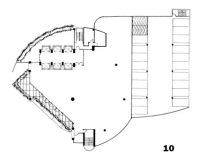

10

11

12

13

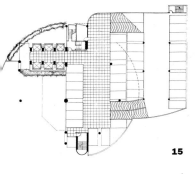

15

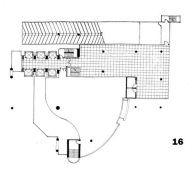

16

17

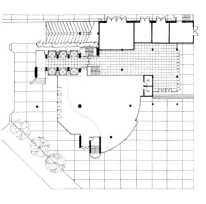

10 Plan: level 4
11 Model showing
landscaped skycourts
12 Section
13 Model showing glass
lift shafts on 'hot' façade
14 Entrance detail
15 Plan: level 3
16 Plan: level 2
17 Model showing services
18 Plan: ground floor

19

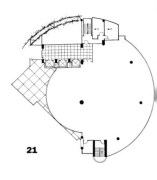

21

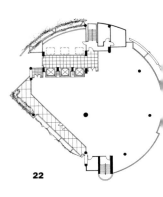

22

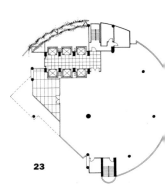

23

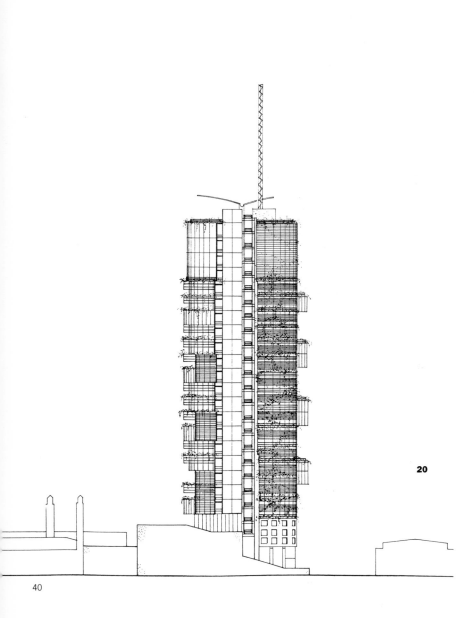

20

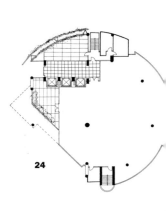

24

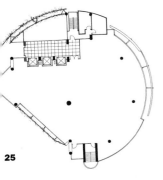

25

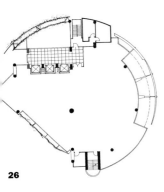

26

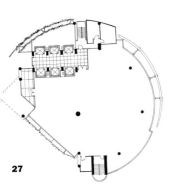

27

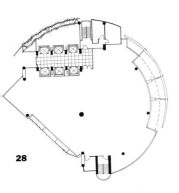

28

29

30

19 Model: bird's-eye view
   from west
20 Elevation
21 Plan: levels 21–24
22 Plan: level 13
23 Plan: level 14
24 Plan: level 5
25 Plan: level 16
26 Plan: level 15
27 Plan: level 6
28 Plan: level 7
29 Model showing skycourts
   and penthouse
30 Location plan

Menara Boustead
1986

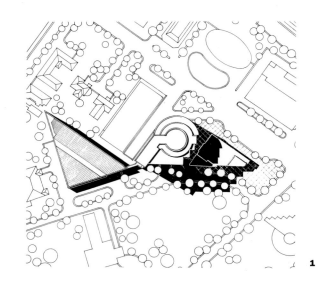

Location
Jalan Raja Chulan, Kuala
Lumpur, Malaysia

Client
Boustead Holdings Bhd

Size
29,840 m² with 15,630 m²
of car parking; 31 storeys

Plot ratio
1:6.97

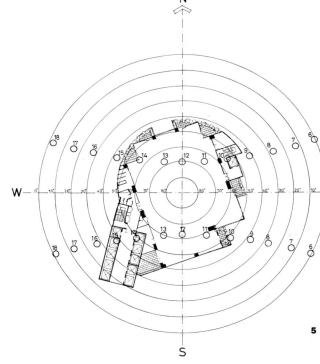

1

2

3

4

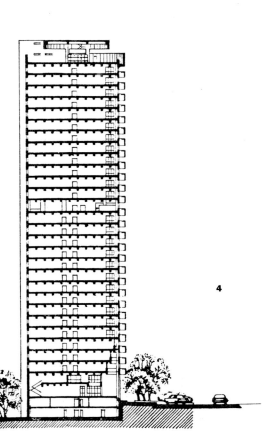

5

The client wanted a corporate headquarters building which had to be completed over a very short period. The project was fast-tracked from design to occupancy.

The intention was to design an office building that was more than a series of stacked multiple enclosed concrete trays. Consequently, terraces or skycourts are located at all corners all the way up the building and constitute a dominant feature. These transitional spaces have a number of functions: they allow the introduction of planting and landscaping in the upper floors; they provide a flexible zone in which, potentially, further services could be located; and they provide adequate sun shading to permit full-height glazing which enhances the quality of natural light and ventilation in the office work spaces. They may also be used to conceal supplementary air-conditioning units.

The building's configuration responds to the tropical sun. It is clad in a ventilated rain-check aluminium skin which traps heat and dissipates it before it can be transmitted to the main structure. Lift cores and toilets are located on the hot west and east sides and lift lobbies have natural light and ventilation. All west- and east-facing windows are sun-shaded.

7

M
E
N
A
R
A

B
O
U
S
T
E
A
D

8

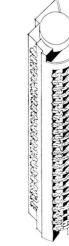

9

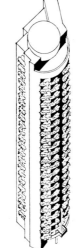

1 Site plan
2 Balconies over entrance
3 The planted façade
4 Section
5 Sunpath diagram
6 View of planting
7 Underside of entrance
8 Planted skycourts
  climbing the façade
9 Study sketches

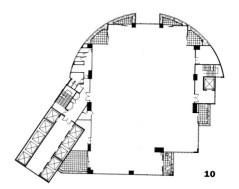

10

11

12

13

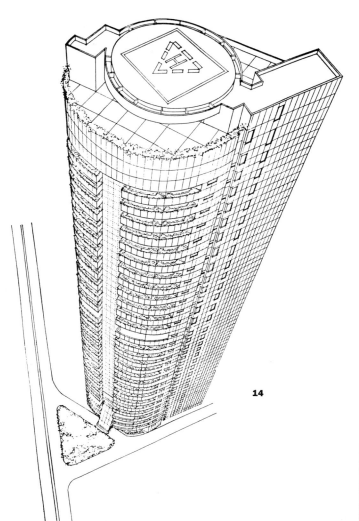

14

15

10 Plan: typical floor
11 Full-height ventilation-
controlling glazing onto
balcony
12 Sun-shaded balcony
13 Irrigation system
14 Axonometric view
15 Naturally lit lift lobby
16 General view

1. UNPROTECTED CURTAIN WALL

UNPROTECTED GLAZING

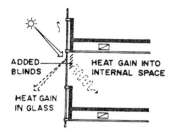

ADDED BLINDS

HEAT GAIN INTO INTERNAL SPACE

HEAT GAIN IN GLASS

2. DEEP RECESSES AND BALCONIES

RECESSED GLAZING AND BALCONIES

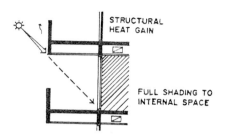

STRUCTURAL HEAT GAIN

FULL SHADING TO INTERNAL SPACE

3. RECESSED WINDOWS

RECESSED WINDOWS

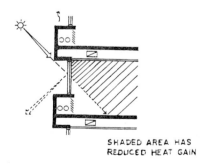

SHADED AREA HAS REDUCED HEAT GAIN

4. HORIZONTAL FINS

HORIZONTAL FINS

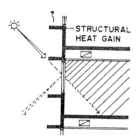

STRUCTURAL HEAT GAIN

5. VERTICAL FINS

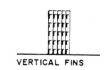

VERTICAL FINS

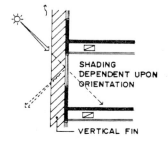

SHADING DEPENDENT UPON ORIENTATION

VERTICAL FIN

6. DEEP RECESSES COMBINED WITH BALCONY TERRACES, PLANTERS, HEAT-SINK CLADDING

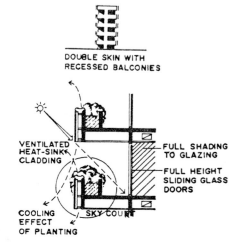

DOUBLE SKIN WITH RECESSED BALCONIES

VENTILATED HEAT-SINK CLADDING

FULL SHADING TO GLAZING

FULL HEIGHT SLIDING GLASS DOORS

COOLING EFFECT OF PLANTING

SKY COURT

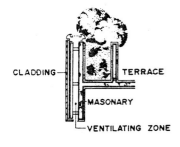

CLADDING — TERRACE

MASONARY

VENTILATING ZONE

18

19

20

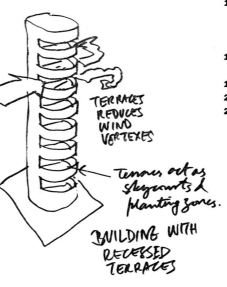

SMOOTH SKIN BUILDING

BUILDING WITH COOLING-FINS (ENGINE-CYLINDER COOLING FINS ANALOGY)

BUILDING WITH RECESSED TERRACES

TERRACES REDUCES WIND VORTEXES

Terraces act as skycourts & planting zones.

17 Principles and details of the development of low-energy shading (drawing by Noraini Bte Ahmad)
18 Cladding detail showing ventilation zone
19 General view
20 Planting
21 Wind-study sketches

47

IBM Plaza
1983–1985

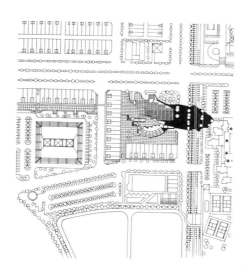

1

Location
Taman Tun Dr Ismail, Kuala
Lumpur, Malaysia

Client
TTDI Development Sdn Bhd

Size
26,000 m² with
15,800 m² of car parking;
52 m² Hawkers' Centre;
24 storeys

Plot ratio
1:4.106

2

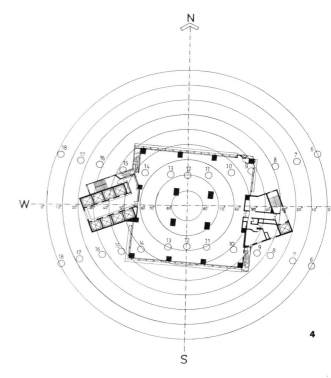

3

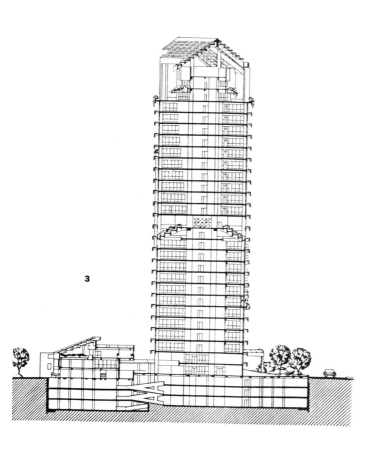

4

The developers commissioned a design that would reflect the progressive nature of the company. The building is a 24-storey office tower linked by a curvilinear bridge to a two-storey restaurant/food court block. The two forms are juxtaposed in a plaza. Surrounding roads are pedestrianized and paved to meet adjoining shophouses.

Two geometries are bioclimatically acknowledged – that of the sun's path and that of the context, specifically the relationship of the site to the road. Typical floors are aligned north–south, that is, relating to the path of the sun. The services cores are on the east and west (the hot) sides and follow the geometry of the site. This configuration of the built forms is a response in planning terms to the local tropical climate.

The top of the tower is pitched – an evocative reminder of the traditional Malay house form. The local landscaping and planting are introduced in an innovative vertical escalating system of planter-boxes and trellises which start from a mound at the ground floor and rise diagonally up the face of the building. At mid-level, these planters traverse horizontally across the breeze-way floor and escalate again diagonally up the other face of the building to the roof terraces.

The ground floor entrance lift lobby leading to the plaza is open to the outside environment and is naturally ventilated. Upper floors are extended in an asymmetrical pattern resulting in wedge-shaped projections and an overall form which is irregular, a deviation from the Modernist slab form for towers. While the configuration of the floor plan here differs from that of the Menara Boustead, the bioclimatic principles are similar.

I B M   P L A Z A (vertical text on right)

I
B
M

P
L
A
Z
A

6

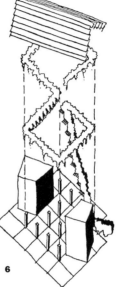

7

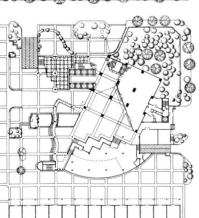

8

1 Site plan
2 General view
3 Section
4 Sunpath diagram
5 Ground-floor plaza
6 Study sketch
7 Plan: ground floor
8 Balconies and planters cutting across the face of the building

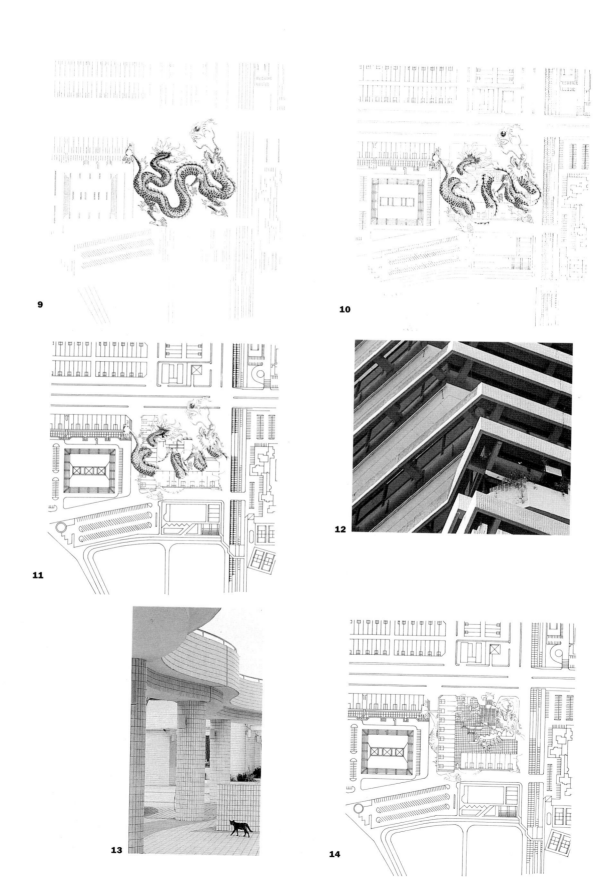

9

10

11

12

13

14

9   Conceptual plan: A
10   Conceptual plan: B
11   Conceptual plan: C
      (drawings by Raymond
      Soh)
12   Skewed balconies at
      corner
13   The plaza
14   Conceptual plan: D
15   View from south-west

16

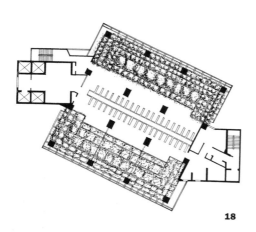

18

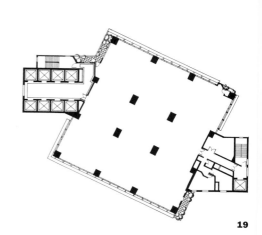

19

20

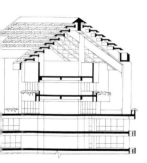

21

22

23   **25**

24

16 Planted balconies
17 Shading provided by deep
recesses
18 Plan: typical floor
19 Plan: 11th floor
20 View showing pitched roof
21 Detail showing filter roof
22 Planter detail
23 View of plaza
24 Detail of bridge
25 View of ground floor

Plaza Atrium
1981–1986

Location
Jalan P. Ramlee, Kuala
Lumpur, Malaysia

Client
Ban Seng Development
Sdn Bhd

Size
10,700 m²; 24 storeys

Plot ratio
1:5.07

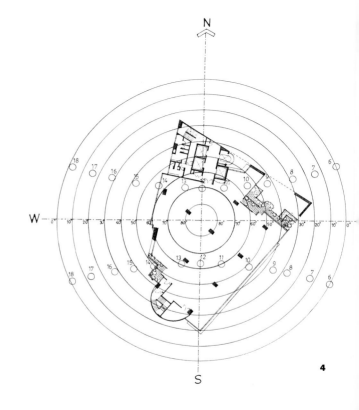

The Plaza Atrium is a landmark commercial building for sale and rental. With a restricted site, it uses almost the maximum permitted plot ratio. The ground and first floors are for retail or bank use, with car parking integrated with the built form, and offices from the second floor up.

The building's dominant feature is the large semi-enclosed naturally ventilated atrium onto which the cascading terraces of the office floors all face. Unlike most atriums, this space is not located within the building envelope but in the transitional space between the interior and the exterior. The atrium is capped by a louvered roof using Z-profile louvres. This filters out rain while allowing hot air from within the atrium to flow out and diffused sunlight to enter. The entire atrium acts as a giant wind scoop, capturing airflow high up on the building and enabling wind to enter the typical upper floors, controlled by the sliding doors of the terraces facing the atrium void.

The office floors facing onto the atrium are set back and lined with landscaped terraces with views down into the atrium space.

P
L
A
Z
A

A
T
R
I
U
M

6

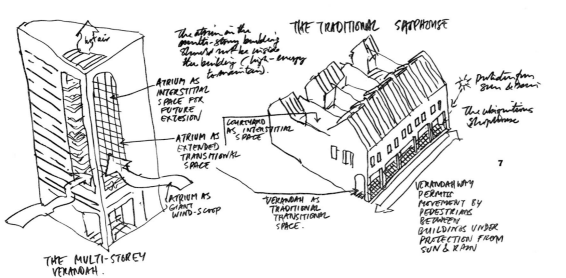

THE TRADITIONAL SHOPHOUSE

THE MULTI-STOREY VERANDAH.

1 General view
2 Site plan
3 View of semi-enclosed atrium
4 Sunpath diagram
5 Distant view
6 Detail of atrium at upper levels
7 Comparative study sketch

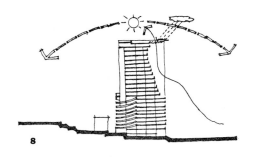

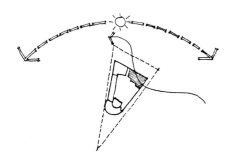

8

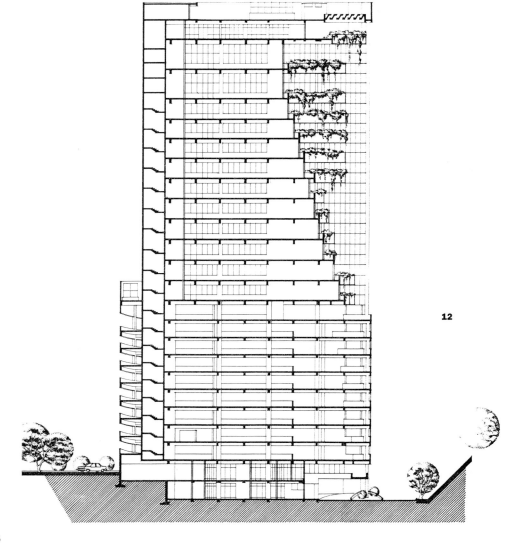

12

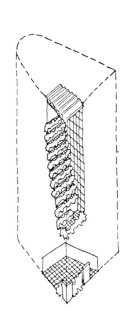

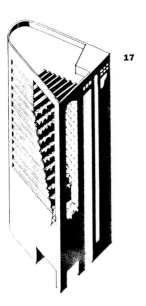

15

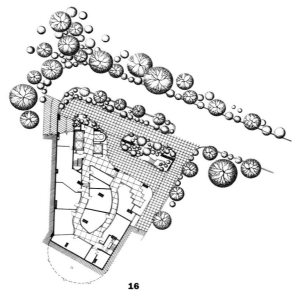

14

16

17

18

8 Shading study
9 Shading study (drawn by Tan Kuce Ten)
10 Detail of balconies
11 Detail of balconies and structure
12 Section
13 Planting study sketch
14 View of atrium
15 View looking down on atrium
16 Plan: ground floor
17 Axonometric showing planting in atrium
18 Plan: typical floor

Menara Mesiniaga
1989–1992

1

Location
Subang Jaya, Selangor
Malaysia

Client
Mesiniaga Sdn Bhd

Size
10,340 m² gross
(6741 m² net) with 404 m²
of car parking; 15 storeys
plus one basement level

Plot ratio
1:6

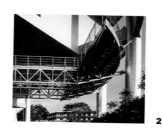

2

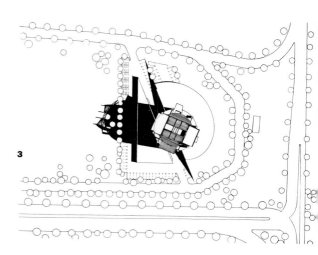

3

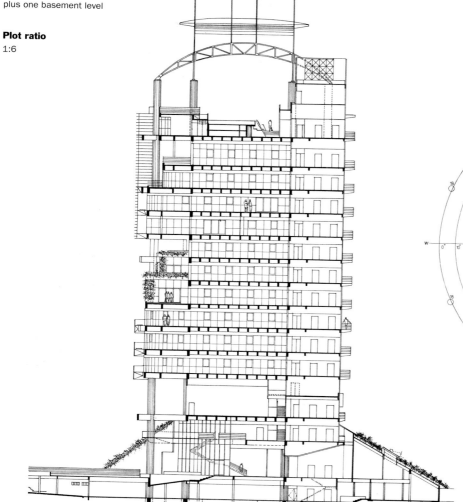

4

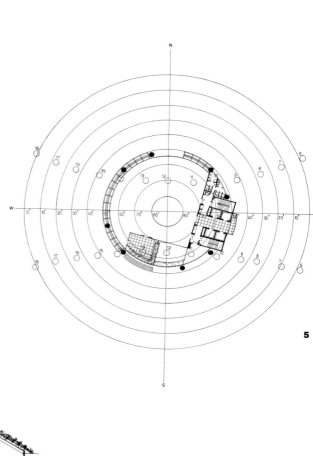

5

This is a headquarters building for an electronics and business machine company (IBM's Malaysia agency). Both external and internal design features use a bioclimatic approach to produce an operationally low-energy building that makes the most of the pleasant ambient tropical climate.

The most striking design feature is the planting which is introduced into the façade and the 'skycourts', starting from a three-storey-high planted mound and spiralling up the face of the building. Triple-height recessed terraces towards the upper part of the building are also planted. These atriums enable the channelling of a cool flow of air throughout the building's transitional spaces while the planting provides shade and an oxygen-rich atmosphere.

Curtain wall glazing is used only on the north and south façades to moderate solar gain. All the window areas facing the hot east and west faces have external aluminium fins and louvres to provide sun shading. Glazing details allow the light-green glass to act as a ventilation filter, protecting the interior without totally insulating it. Terraces are provided for all the office floors, and have sliding full-height glass doors to control the extent of natural ventilation (when required). Lift lobbies, stairwells and toilets have natural ventilation and sunlight. The lift lobbies do not need pressurisation for fire protection.

The roof-top sun terrace is covered with a sunroof of trussed steel and aluminium; this shades and filters light on to the swimming pool and the curved gymnasium roof (it also provides space for the possible future fixing of solar cells). Internally, enclosed rooms are placed as a central core rather than being situated at the periphery. This ensure good natural lighting and views out for the peripherally located workstations. Because the building is circular in plan, there are no dark corners.

The building employs a range of automated systems to reduce energy consumption by equipment and the air-conditioning plant.

 **8**

 **9**

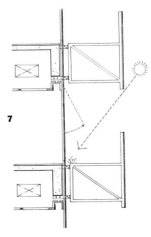

7

1 Sun shading
2 Entrance detail
3 Site plan
4 East–west section
5 Sunpath diagram
6 Model
7 Sun-shading details
8 Detail of void
9 View out to terrace
10 Detail of balconies

10

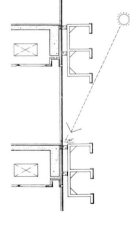

11

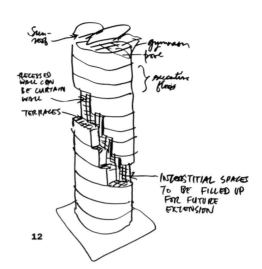

12

13

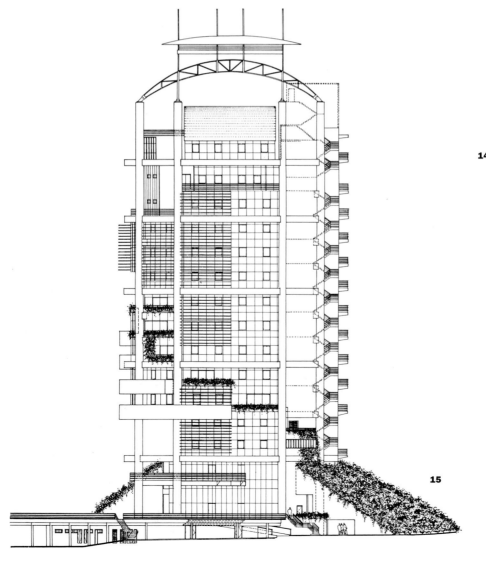

15

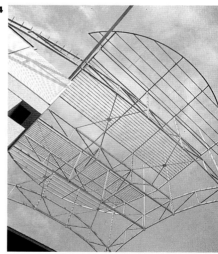

14

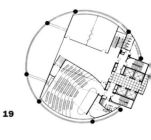

19

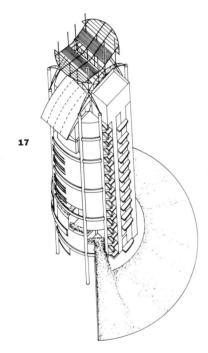

17

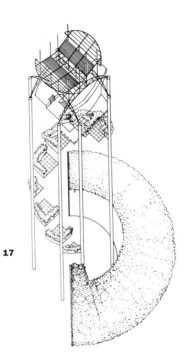

17

18

11 View of skycourt
12 Sketch study
13 General view
14 Shading structure on roof
15 South-west elevation
16 Detail of shading
   structure
17 Sketches showing the
   built form, and planting
   and terraces
18 View showing the planted
   ramp
19 Plan: 1st floor
20 Plan: 2nd floor
21 Plan: 4th floor
22 Plan: 7th floor

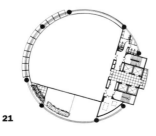

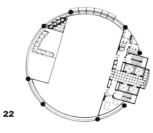

21

22

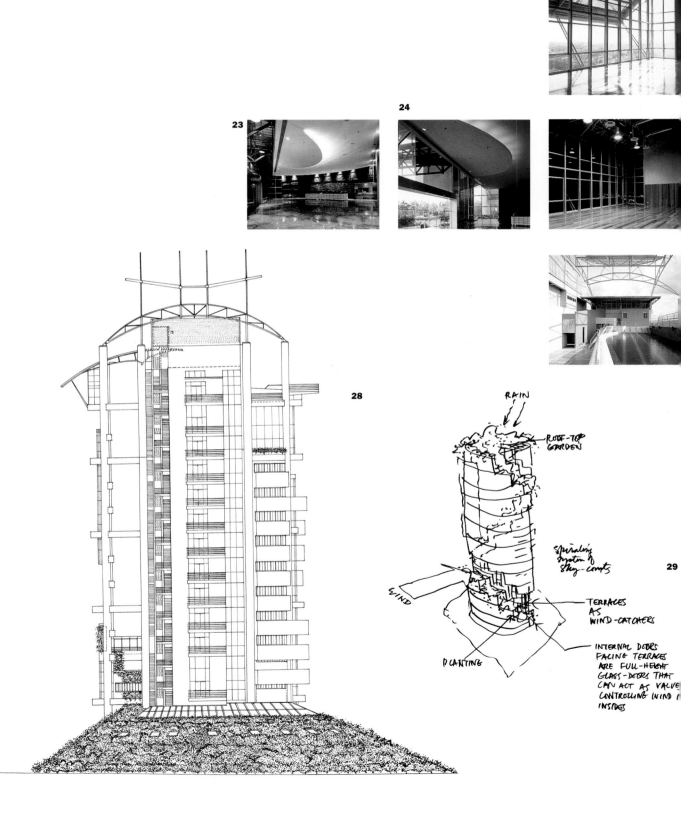

23

24

28

29

RAIN

ROOF-TOP
GARDEN

Spiraling
system of
sky-courts

WIND

TERRACES
AS
WIND-CATCHERS

PLANTING

INTERNAL DOORS
FACING TERRACES
ARE FULL-HEIGHT
GLASS-DOORS THAT
CAN ACT AS VALVE
CONTROLLING WIND
INSIDES

23 The lobby at night
24 Lobby detail
25 View from the gymnasium by day
26 View from the gymnasium by night
27 Terrace with pool
28 East elevation
29 Concept sketch
30 View of skycourts
31 Plan: 8th floor
32 Plan: 11th floor
33 Plan: 12th upper floor

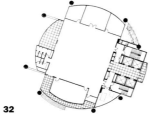

32

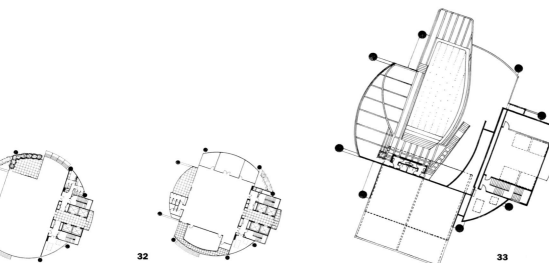

33

Central Plaza
1992–1995

Location
Jalan Sultan Ismail, Kuala
Lumpur, Malaysia

Client
Malview Sdn Bhd

Size
31,250 m² gross; 27 storeys

Plot ratio
1:10.5

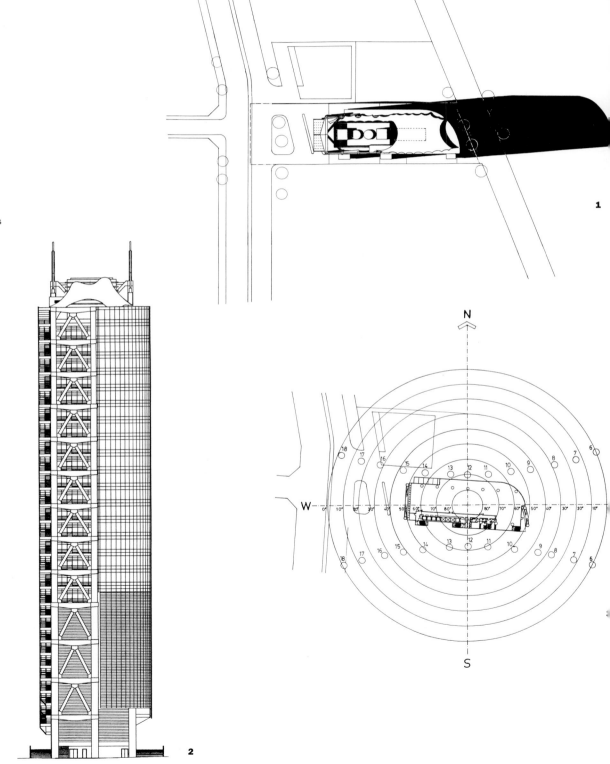

1

2

The brief called for a landmark office building for sale and rental, maximizing the plot ratio. The lower ground floor houses a restaurant while the ground floor and mezzanine are for shops or bank use. More than 14,000 square metres of car parking are located above ground.

The building's dominant feature is its structural bracing system which makes possible internally column-free floors, preferred for marketing reasons. The V-shaped cross-bracing of the external columns on the east and west sides provide bracing for this exceptionally slender tower as well as some sun shading to these faces.

The rectangular site has the ideal east–west orientation. However, the west façade faces an important street and this entailed putting marketable windows on this hot face. To provide sun shading, the west façade is set back behind the structural frame.

The north-east wall, which provides good views of the distant Ampang Hills, is curved and glazed with solar-reflective glass. Balconies are provided on the east façade: these give shade and serve as sky terraces. Terraces with planters also feature on the north face, which step up to the roof terrace. Lift cores, stairways and toilets have natural ventilation and light.

4

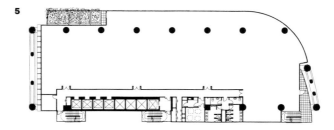

5

6

1 Site plan
2 East elevation
3 Sunpath diagram
4 Model: west elevation
5 Typical floor plan: 12th–23rd floors
6 Elevation of entrance foyer (drawn by Rachel Atthis)

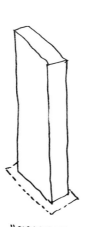

"CIGARETTE PACK" SLIM FARM

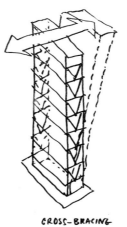

7

CROSS-BRACING TO REDUCE COLUMNS AT CENTER OF OFFICE FLOOR

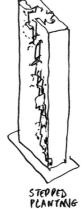

STEPPED PLANTING

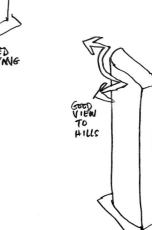

GOOD VIEW TO HILLS

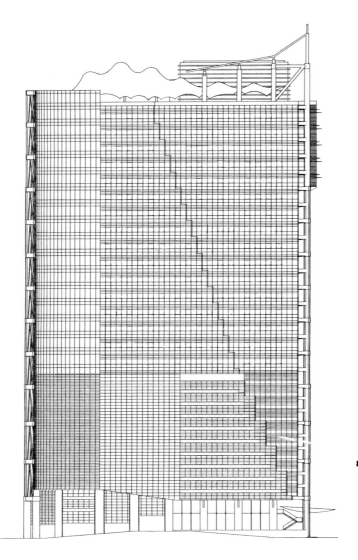

8

9

7 Concept sketches
8 South elevation
9 Model: south elevation
10 Model: general view

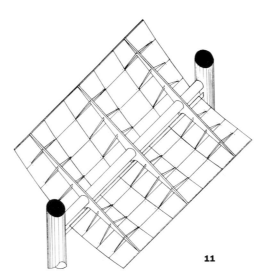

11

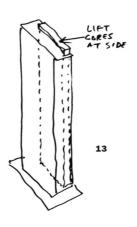

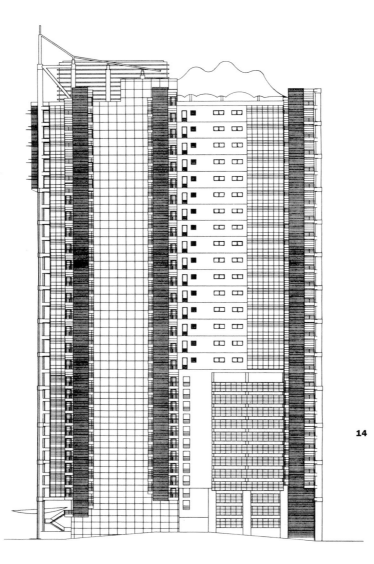

14

LIFT CORES AT SIDE

13

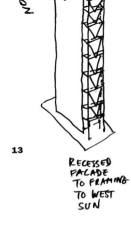

13

RECESSED
FACADE
TO FRAMING
TO WEST
SUN

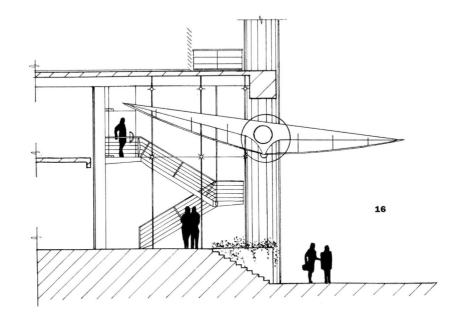

16

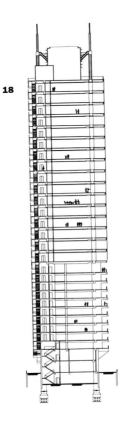

18

19

20

21

11 Entrance foyer canopy

12 Model from the south-east

13 Concept sketches

14 North elevation

15 Model from the south-west

16 Section: entrance foyer canopy

17 Section

18 Short section

19 Plan view of model

20 Model: detail of upper floors

21 Model: detail showing bracing and entrance canopy

Budaya Tower
1992–1996

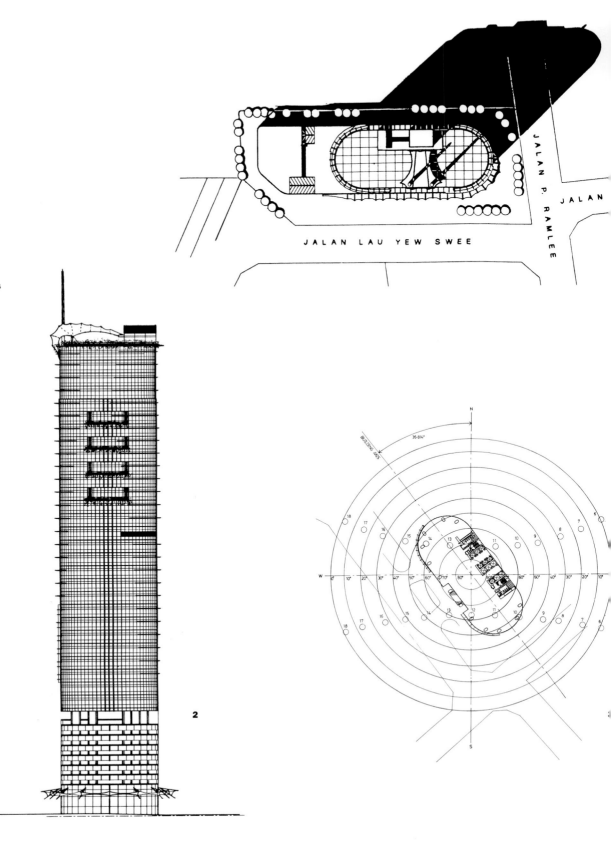

Location
Kuala Lumpur, Malaysia

Client
ERF Properties Sdn Bhd

Size
43,888 m² gross
(34,217 m² net); 37 storeys

Plot ratio
1:9

2

The rectangular site is orientated diagonally north–south and the site conditions are such that the geometry of the site and that of the sun path do not coincide. To overcome the difficulties of the site, a capsule-shaped floor plan with semi-circular ends is used. This form geometrically reduces the length of the north–south and east–west external walls, and hence the direct insolation.

Sun shading is placed diagonally to the north-west and south-east faces of the building. This shading takes the form of an extended horizontal fin on all floors except for the lower floors which have 'egg-crate' shaped shading. The top floor contains a naturally ventilated communal space covered with a fabric structure. The ground floor – an 'open to the sky' space extending to a mezzanine floor – is also naturally ventilated.

The dominant feature of the design is the extended semi-enclosed atrium on the south side, expressed by exposed twin columns and steel balconies.

The environmentally responsive external skin has full-height glazing on the diagonal north and south corners. The other corner faces have a louvered sun-shade system but the building opens out to a transitional space facing south-west as an atrium. Off the atrium are landscaped skycourts as events that happen at various levels up the building. Lift lobbies, toilets and stairwells are all naturally ventilated and lit and are located on one of the hot sides of the building.

A BUILDING WITH A RECTANGULAR SHAPE WILL GET SUN ON ALL FACES

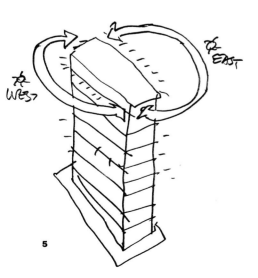

5

6

1 Site plan
2 South-east elevation
3 Sunpath diagram
4 Model showing semi-enclosed atrium
5 Concept sketch
6 Bird's-eye view of model

CAPSULE SHAPED
BUILDING WILL
HAVE OPTIMUM FLOOR
AREA AND EFFICIENT
EXTERNAL WALL AREA
BUT HAS NORTH & SOUTH
FACES THAT WILL NOT
GET DIRECT SOLAR
INSOLATION

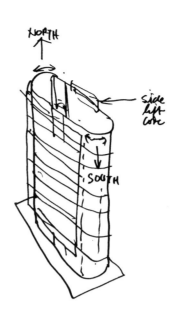

8

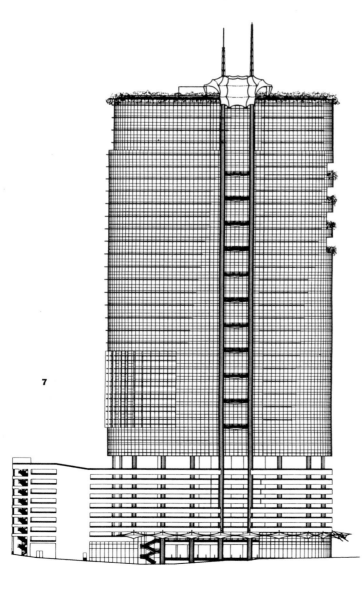

7

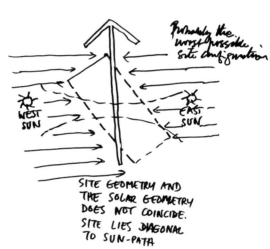

SITE GEOMETRY AND
THE SOLAR GEOMETRY
DOES NOT COINCIDE.
SITE LIES DIAGONAL
TO SUN-PATH

8

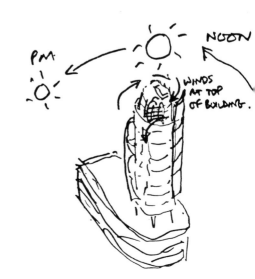

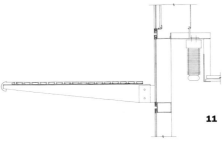

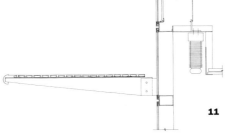

10

11

12

7 South-west elevation
8 Concept sketches (drawn by Paul Matthews)
9 Model: detail of atrium
10 Model showing environmentally interactive skin
11 Sun-shading detail
12 Plan: ground floor

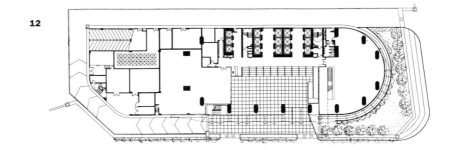

I AM

NSHADING
EAST + WESTSIDES.

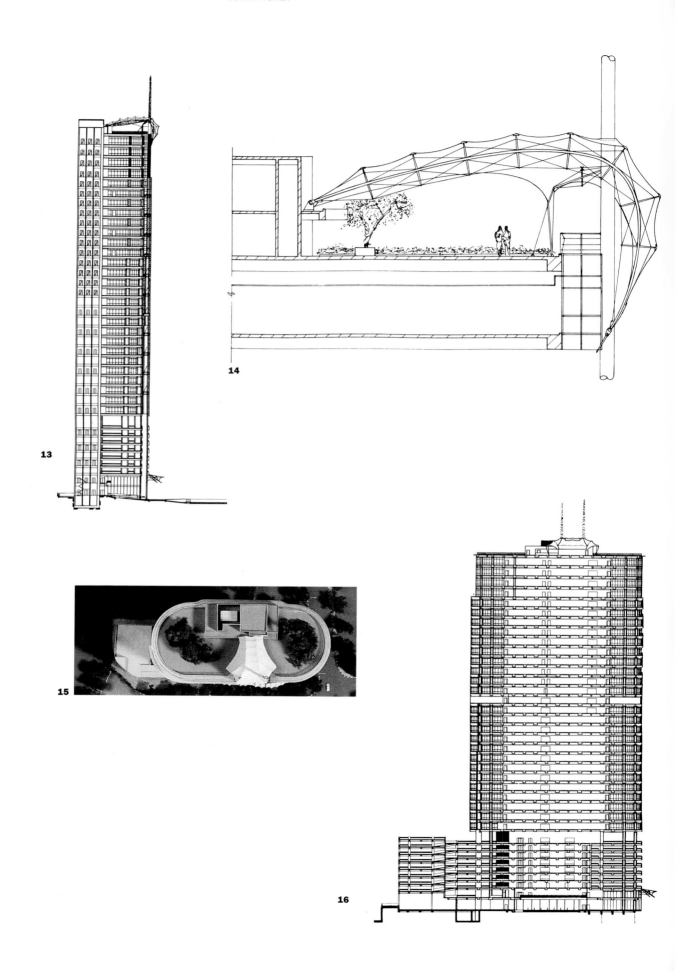

13

14

15

16

13 Short section
14 Rooftop canopy detail
   (drawn by Yeoh Yim
   Seong)
15 Plan view of model
16 Long section
17 General view of model

17

Autumnland Tower
1991–

Location:

Kuala Lumpur, Malaysia

Size:

15,093 m² gross
(10,857 m² net) with
7568 m² of car parking; 24
storeys (plus five basements)

Plot ratio:

1:8

1

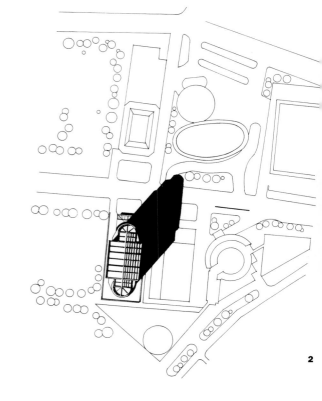

2

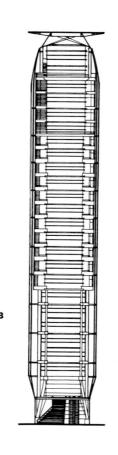

3

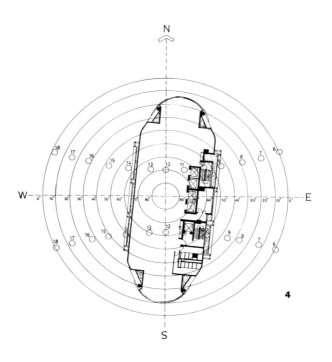

4

The difficult site means that the long sides of the building have to face east and west. To reduce the heat load on these façades a system of moveable louvres and glass panels form an environmentally active skin. The north and south faces have curtain-wall glazing. The lift lobbies are located on the hot east side and are naturally ventilated, as are the stairways and toilets.

5

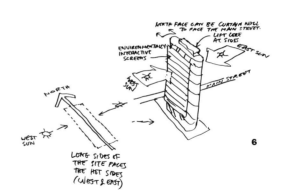

6

1 Computer model: view from north west
2 Site plan
3 North elevation
4 Sunpath diagram
5 Model: from north-west
6 Sketch showing the relationship between the building's screened long façades and the sun
7 Bird's-eye view of the tower in context

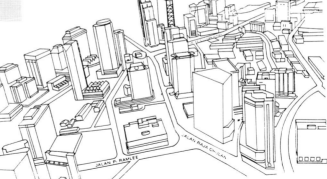

7

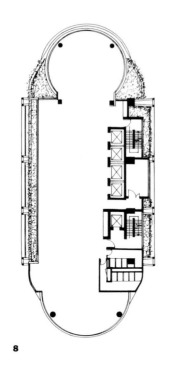

8

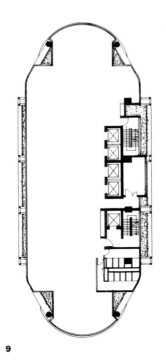

9

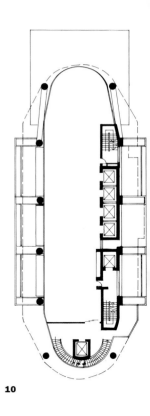

10

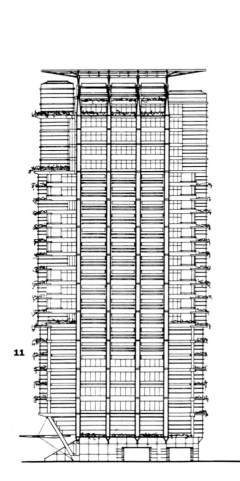

11

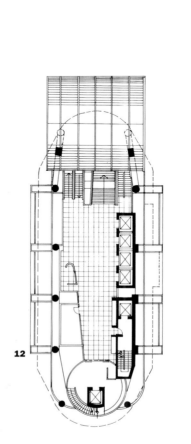

12

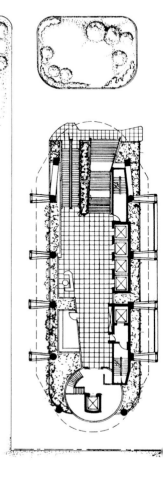

13

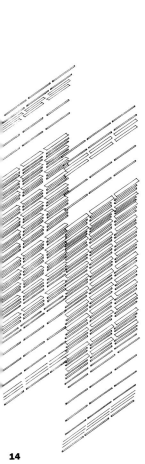

14

15

8 Plan: 18th–21st floors
9 Plan: 9th–17th floors
10 Plan: 2nd–7th floors
11 West elevation
12 Plan: 1st floor
13 Plan: ground floor
14 Sun shades for east and
west façades
15 Model viewed from west

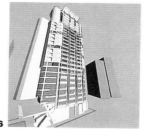

16

17

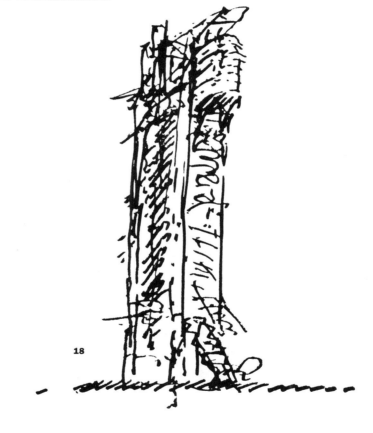

18

19

20

21

22

16 Computer model: the
   west façade
17 Model viewed from the
   north-west
18 Study sketch
19 Computer model: the
   north, street façade
20 Model viewed from the
   north-west
21 Model: the west façade
22 Perspective view

Orchid Tower

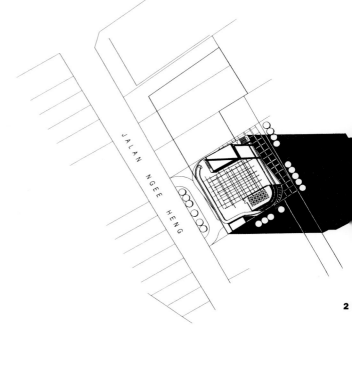

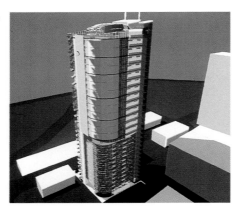

Location
Johor Bahru, Johor, Malaysia

Client
Orchid Hotel Sdn Bhd

Size
108,170 m² gross, 24 storeys
(with basement)

Plot ratio
1:8.3

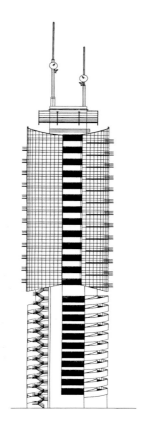

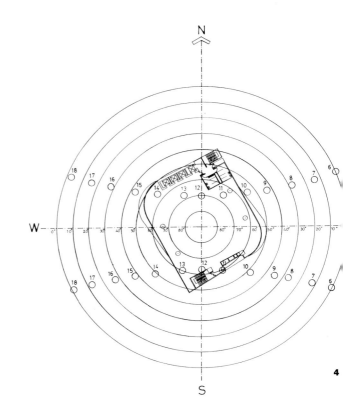

The external walls extend the ideas and the research work on the environmentally responsive wall into a combined external wall design with a variable glazing-detail profile that combines sun shading with a unitized glazing system (on the sides of the building that need solar protection), tapering to butt-jointed glazing on the south side.

Skycourts are located at the upper parts of the tower. These are linked by a secondary staircase to the penthouse roof. There is no built-in air-conditioning, but the balconies can be used for locating individual package air-conditioning condensors if they are required.

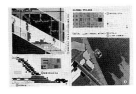

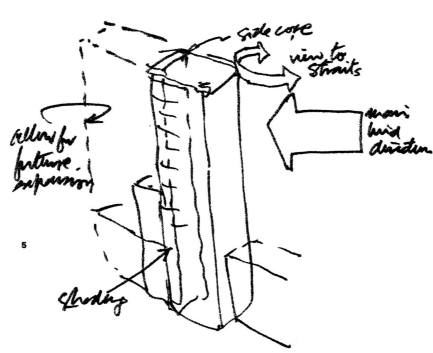

5

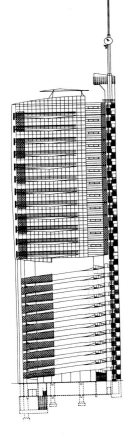

6

7

1 Computer model: view
   from north
2 Site plan
3 South-east elevation
4 Sunpath diagram
5 Concept sketch
6 North-east elevation
7 Computer model:
   entrance

8

9

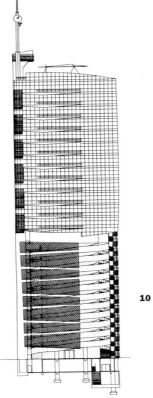

10

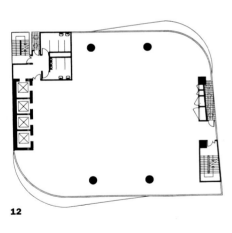

11

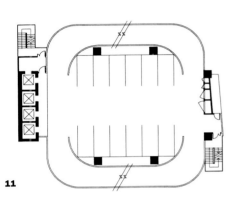

12

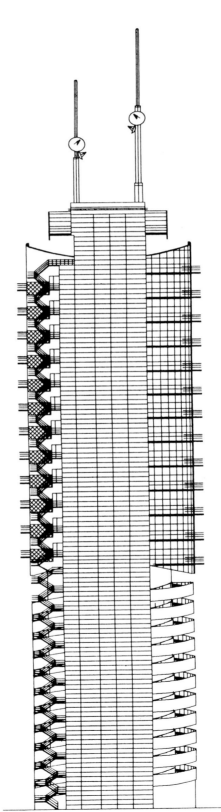

13

8 Computer model showing
environmentally
responsive walls
9 Computer model viewed
from the south
10 South-west elevation
11 Plan: typical car parking:
1st–11th floors
12 Typical floor plan:
12th–23rd floors
13 North-west elevation

MBf Tower
1990–1993

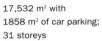

Location:
Jalan Sultan Ahmad Shah,
Penang, Malaysia

Client:
MBf Holdings Bhd

Size:
17,532 m² with
1858 m² of car parking;
31 storeys

1

2

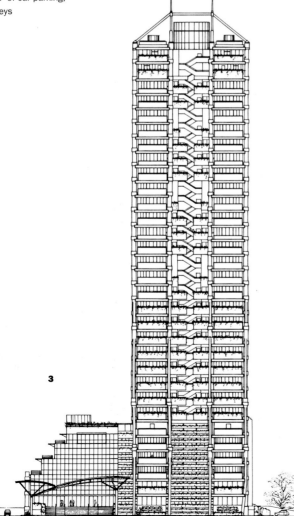

3

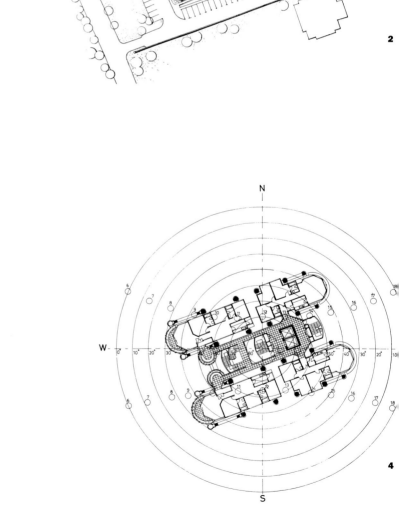

4

This tower is a development of the 'places in the sky' idea. The site is oriented roughly north–south. The MBf tower replaces an earlier demolished multi-storey apartment block by another architect, construction of which was halted when the foundations were found to be faulty. The new project consists of a podium for offices and a banking hall, with 68 luxury apartments in the tower block.

Each residential floor has four apartments separated from the access walkways by air gaps. These increase opportunities for all-round cross ventilation to each apartment unit. The lower apartment units are extended towards the front of the building, creating an internalized atrium facing the swimming-pool deck.

The upper parts of the tower have large, two-storey skycourts for ventilation and planting, and to provide terraces. Lift lobbies are naturally ventilated, with bridges as walkways to the apartments. Stepped planter boxes are located on the building's main façade.

M
B
F

T
O
W
E
R

5

6

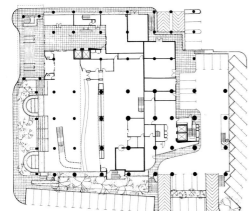

1 The tower under construction
2 Site plan
3 Front elevation
4 Sunpath diagram
5 Model: front elevation
6 Model: west elevation
7 Ground floor plan

8

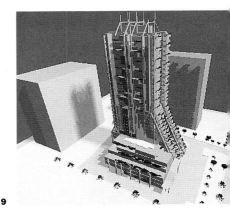

9

10

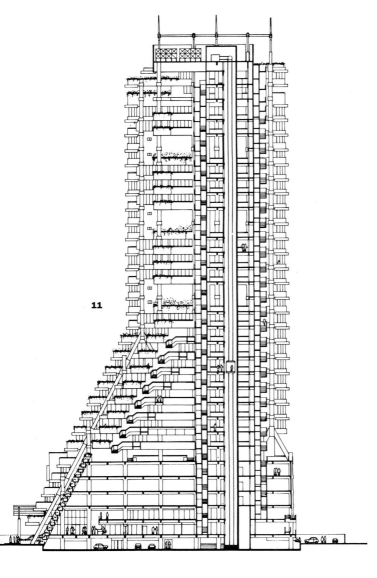

11

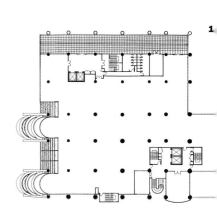

1

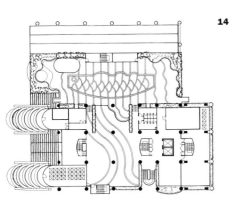

14

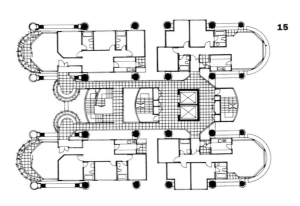

15

8 Computer model showing
stepped planting
9 Computer model showing
office podium
10 Computer model from the
front
11 Section
12 Typical office floor plan:
3rd–5th floors
13 Model: plan view
14 Plan: 6th floor
15 Typical plan: 7th–29th
floors

BP Tower
1992–

Location
Damansara, Kuala Lumpur,
Malaysia

Main tenant
British Petroleum

Size
11,900 m² gross; 15 storeys

Plot ratio
1:3

1

2

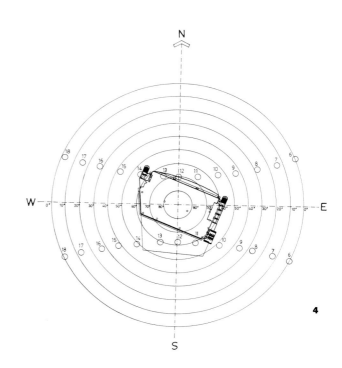

3

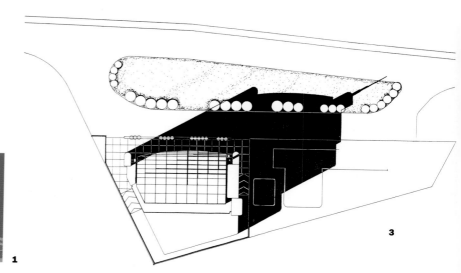

4

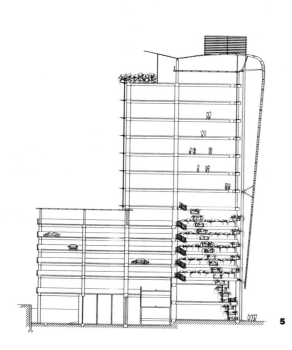

5

The tower is located on the city's edge, relocating offices from the central business district. The design features continuous vertical planting on the front face, stepping up the façade into a court on top of the car-park floors. The planting, besides contributing to the greening of the building, softens the impact of the car park facing the highway.

The main elevation of the site is located at a diagonal to the sunpath. Therefore it receives some early morning sun from the east for part of the year but no sun for the rest of it. In search of a more articulated response to the sunpath, the main façade is curved slightly and its profile has a greater density of sun-shading devices as it curves towards the north-east. At the point where it faces almost due north there are no sun-shading devices and the wall construction is of unitized concealed-frame butt-jointed glazing.

Lift lobbies, stairwells and toilets are naturally ventilated and lit. A filter sunroof over the top storey allows diffused light into the penthouse floors.

7

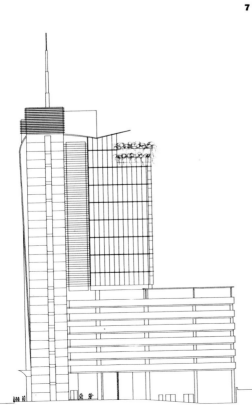

8

1 Computer model: view from north
2 Computer model: view from south
3 Site plan
4 Sunpath diagram
5 South-east elevation
6 Computer model: view from north
7 Perspective
8 North-west elevation

9

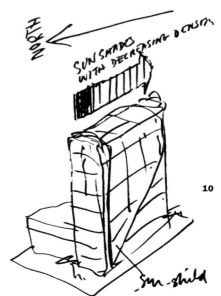

10

9 Computer model: view
from north

10 Concept sketch: sun-
shading

11 Main elevation

11

SCB Tower
1992–

Location
Downtown Kuala Lumpur,
Malaysia

Client
SCB

Size
19,418 m² gross; 25 storeys
(with two basement levels for
car parking)

Plot ratio
1:18.2

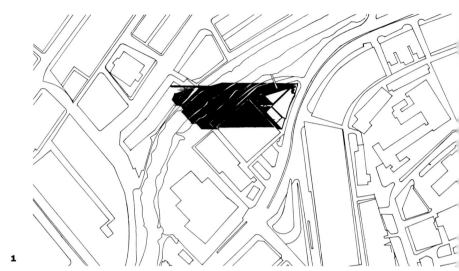

1

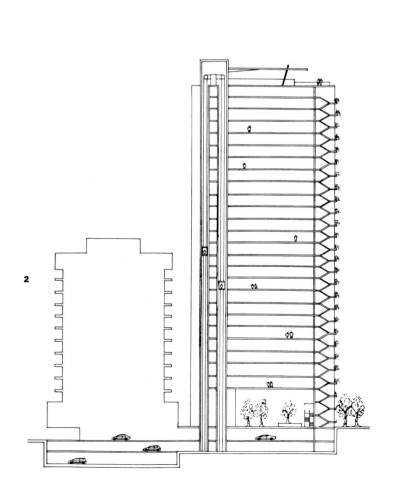

2

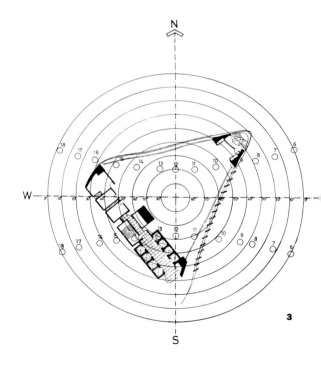

3

The design features a variable curtain wall/clad/sun-shaded profile that wraps around the building. The investigative idea here is for a 'tapering' external wass design. The densest sun shading is on the east side; this tapers to the unshaded north face at the top of the escape stairs. On the west wall, the sun shading comprises automated moveable louvres activated by sensors. The lift lobby, stairs and toilets are naturally ventilated. The open-to-the-sky ground floor acts as a transitional space between the public realm of the street and the river on the north of the site.

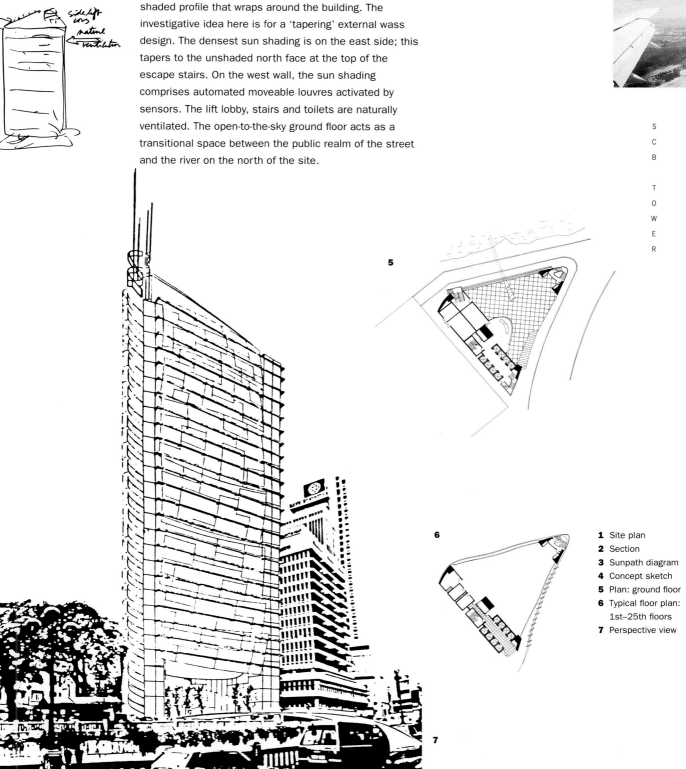

5

6

7

1 Site plan
2 Section
3 Sunpath diagram
4 Concept sketch
5 Plan: ground floor
6 Typical floor plan:
   1st–25th floors
7 Perspective view

1

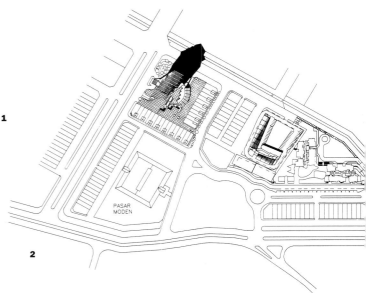

2

Location
Taman Tun Dr Ismail, Kuala
Lumpur, Malaysia

Client
TTDI Development Sdn Bhd

Size
44,840 m², with
21,800 m² of car parking;
28 storeys (two towers)

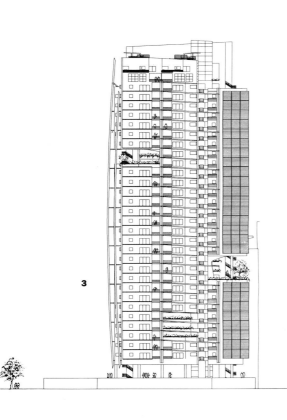

3

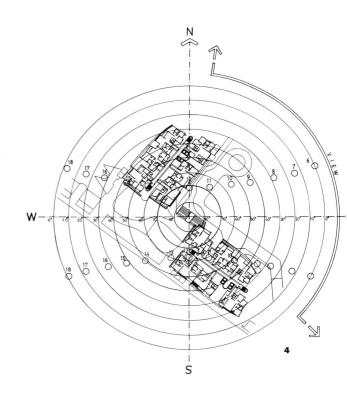

4

This project marks a new stage in the practice's research, design and development programme by exploring the use of high-velocity wind at the upper parts of the tall building for ventilation and energy conservation.

Residential units are designed to have maximum external wall surfaces to increase cross-ventilation and maximize passive cooling. The typical floor plan places each apartment as an individual unit connected by sky bridges and with minimum party walls. Large atriums serving as skycourts are cut out from the façades to give communal green spaces in the air and to increase sunlight penetration and ventilation to the internal bridges and walkways that serve the apartments. The hot east and west external façades employ adjustable sun shades and louvered screens.

'Wind-wing walls' are used to channel wind into ceiling plenums to ventilate the inner rooms of the apartments. Early tests using a wind plane over stairwells to channel air down the staircases proved ineffective and this idea was subsequently rejected.

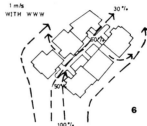

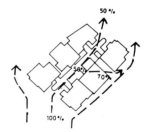

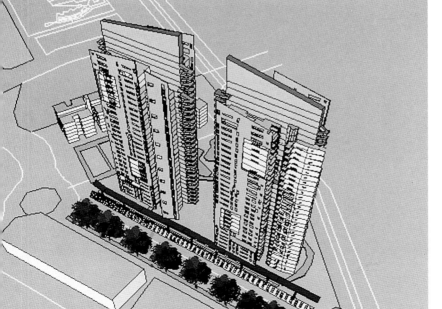

1 Computer model of development
2 Site plan
3 North tower, east elevation
4 Sunpath diagram
5 Model
6 Wing wall analysis
7 Computer model: bird's-eye view

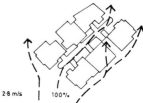

8

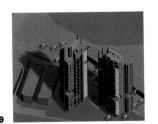

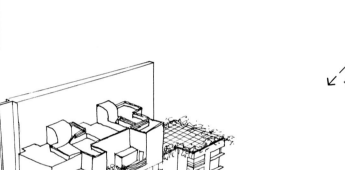

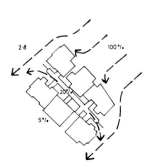

9

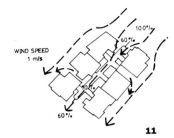

WIND SPEED
1 m/s

100°/°

60°/°

60°/°

11

2 8m/s

100°/°

50°/°

40°/°

50°/°

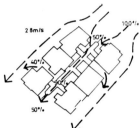

1m/s

100°/°

39°/°

20°/°

8 Model: general view
9 Computer model
10 Computer model
11 Wing wall analysis
12 Axonometric view of study
     model

2·8

100°/°

20°/°

5°/°

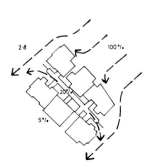

12

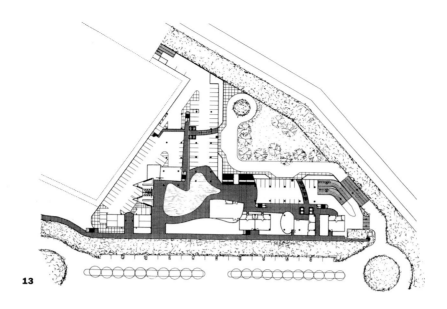

13

14

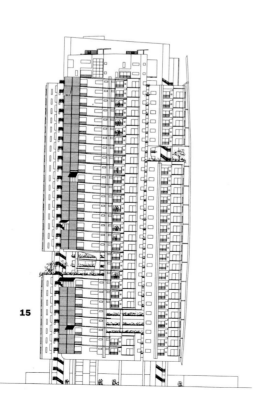

15

16

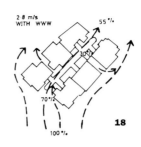

2.8 m/s
WITH WWW

55 %
30 %
70 %
100 %

18

1 m/s
WITHOUT WWW

30 %
80 %
100 %

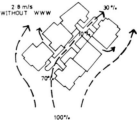

2.8 m/s
WITHOUT WWW

30 %
70 %
100 %

13 Ground floor plan
14 North tower: typical floor plan
15 South tower: north elevation
16 Model: north and south towers
17 Computer model of earlier design option
18 Wing wall analysis
19 Wing wall analysis
20 Wing wall analysis

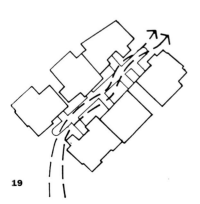

19

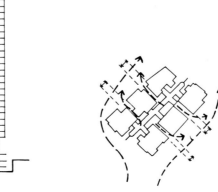

20

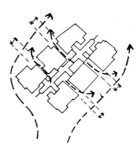

Penggiran Apartment Towers #2
1993–1996

Location

Taman Tun Dr Ismail, Kuala
Lumpur, Malaysia

Client

TTDI Development Sdn Bhd

Size

9 storeys

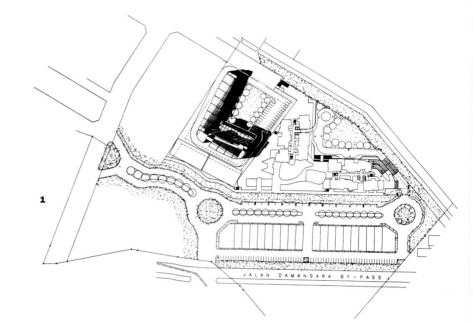

1

JALAN DAMANSARA BY-PASS

2

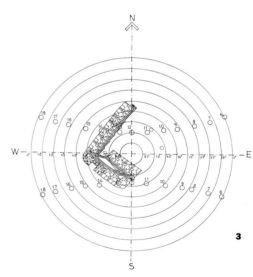

3

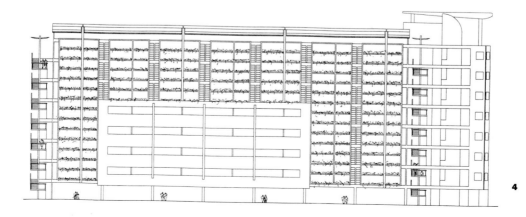

4

The scheme provides 116 low-cost apartments. The plan is single loaded to improve cross ventilation. Where two blocks are back to back, an air gap is provided. A double roof gives solar protection to the top floor. All toilets and kitchens are naturally ventilated.

6

8

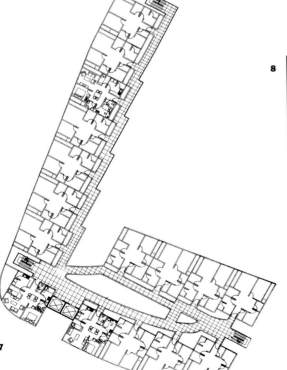

7

1 Site plan
2 Model viewed from east
3 Sunpath diagram
4 West elevation
5 Model viewed from west
6 Axonometric view
7 Typical floor plan
8 Model viewed from south-west

Seacorp Tower
1994–

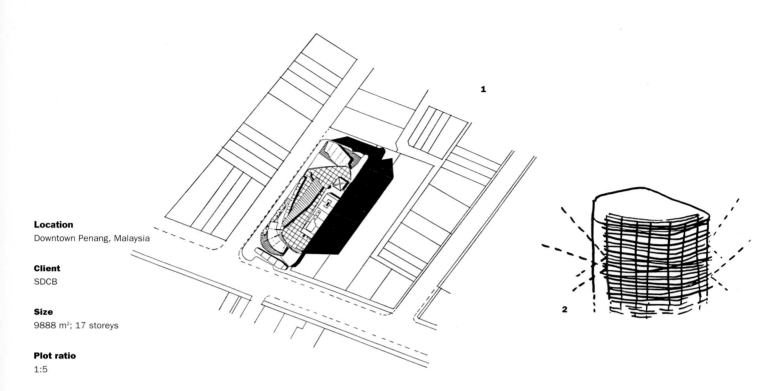

1

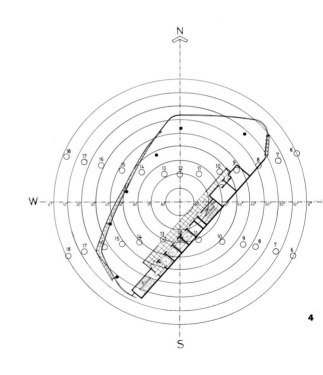

2

Location
Downtown Penang, Malaysia

Client
SDCB

Size
9888 m²; 17 storeys

Plot ratio
1:5

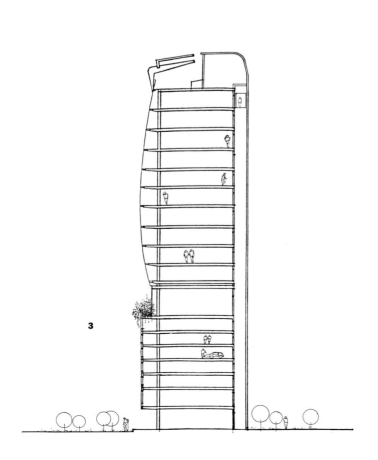

3

4

The building is the corporate headquarters for a financial institution which has apportioned three floors to the landowners. The design features a semi-enclosed public verandahway at ground level, solar shading, skycourts and terraces and naturally ventilated and lit lift lobbies, staircases and toilets.

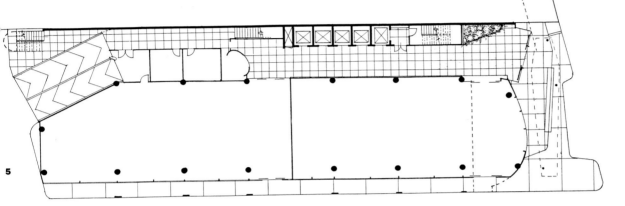

5

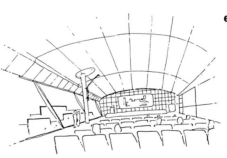

6

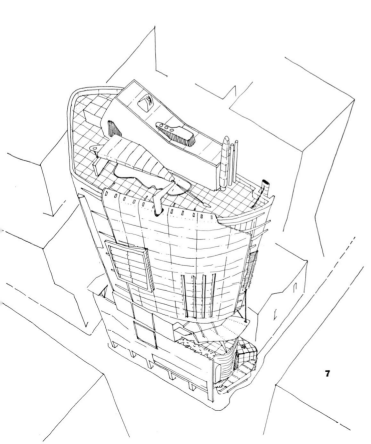

7

1 Site plan
2 Sketch: environmental filter
3 Section
4 Sunpath diagram
5 Ground floor plan
6 View of auditorium (drawn by Ang Chee)
7 Perspective

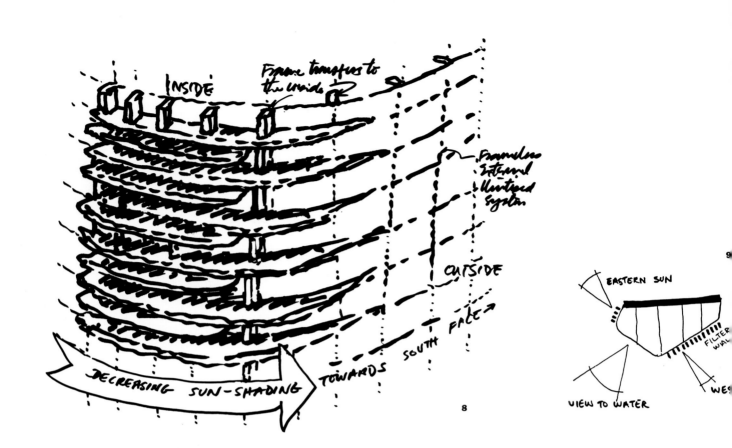

INSIDE

Frame transfers to the inside ?

Frameless External Muntined System

OUTSIDE

DECREASING SUN-SHADING TOWARDS SOUTH FACE →

8

EASTERN SUN

FILTER WALL

VIEW TO WATER

WEST

9

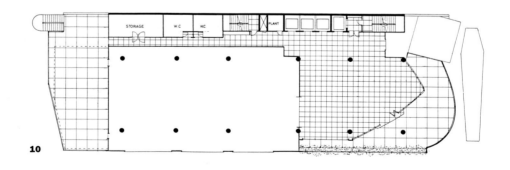

STORAGE W.C WC PLANT

10

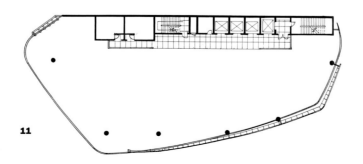

11

12

8 Sunshade concept sketch
9 Orientation sketch
10 Plan: auditorium level
11 Plan: typical office floor
12 View of entrance (drawn
   by Ang Chee)

210 Tower

1

Location
Downtown Kuala Lumpur,
Malaysia

Client
SDCB

Size
25,855 m² gross; 37 storeys

Plot ratio
1:6.75

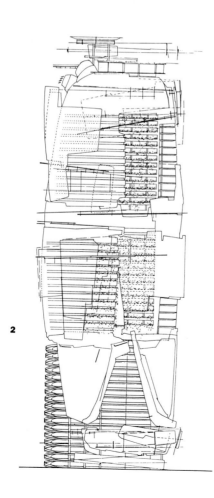

2

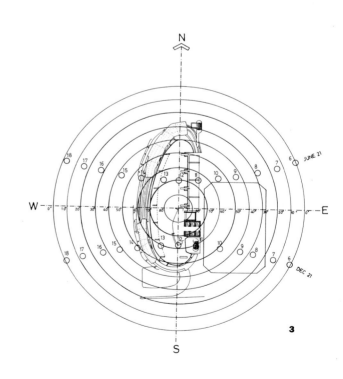

3

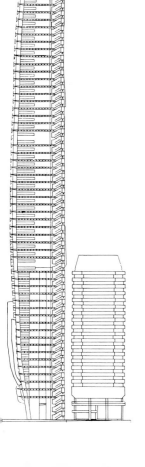

With its longest elevations facing west and east, this is a bioclimatically difficult site. The external wall design explores the vertical layering of a building's façades using a combination of cladding, glazing, shading, balconies and planting.

Lift lobbies, staircases and toilets are naturally ventilated.

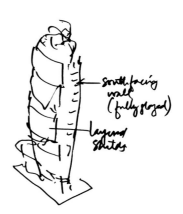

4

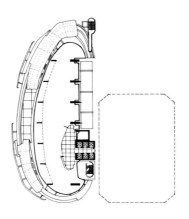

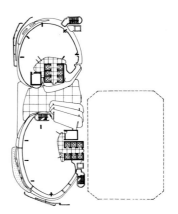

6

5

1 Site plan: options 1 and 2
2 Elevation
3 Sunpath diagram
4 Concept sketches
5 Section
6 Typical floor plans:
  options 1 and 2

Metrolux Tower 1B, Casa del Sol
1992–1994

Location

Bukit Antarabangsa, Selangor,
Malaysia

Client

Metrolux Sendirian Bhd

Size

26,904 m² gross, 11 storeys
(160 apartments)

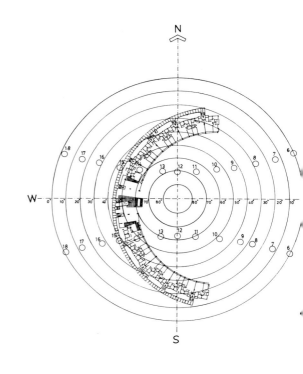

1

2

SKY COURTS

3

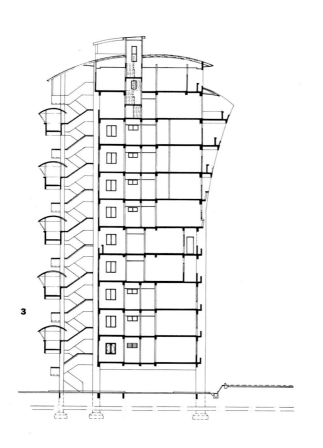

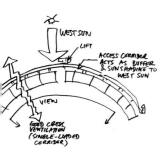

The building form is a semi-circular slab. It features planted and terraced skycourts that are spatially interconnected and placed in a diagonal pattern, stepping sideways from the slab's centre. These skycourts provide terraces for the adjoining residential units. The naturally ventilated single-loaded corridor faces the hot west side of the site and buffers the afternoon sun. The corridor is separated from the tower slab by an air gap. This gives privacy and provides opportunities for cross ventilation through the apartments. All the apartments are designed with through ventilation, and the lift lobbies and staircases that separate the two halves of the curved slab are naturally lit and ventilated.

7

1 Location plan
2 Concept sketch:
   skycourts and balconies
3 Section
4 Sunpath diagram
5 Section
6 Concept sketch: shading
   and cross ventilation
7 Perspective view
8 East elevation

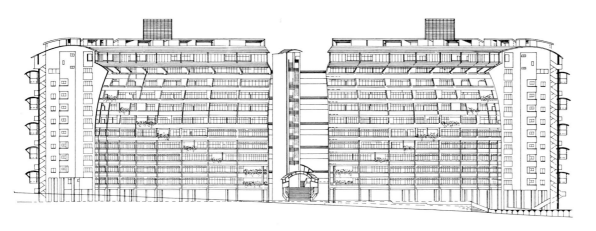

Metrolux Tower 2A, Promenade
1993–

Location
Bukit Antarabangsa, Selangor,
Malaysia

Client
Metrolux Sdn Bhd

Size
23, 367 m² gross, 12 storeys
(160 apartments)

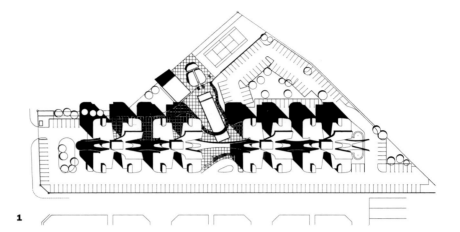

1

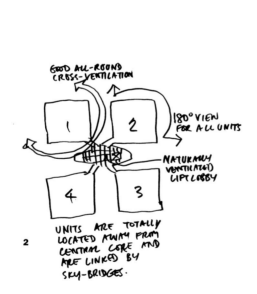

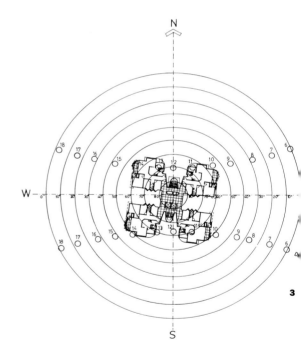

GOOD ALL-ROUND
CROSS-VENTILATION

180° VIEW
FOR ALL UNITS

NATURALLY
VENTILATED
LIFT LOBBY

UNITS ARE TOTALLY
LOCATED AWAY FROM
CENTRAL CORE AND
ARE LINKED BY
SKY-BRIDGES.

2

3

4

The complex's towers are aligned over a central semi-enclosed deck that serves as a social-interaction promenade for residents. On one side this promenade fans out to a pool deck with other recreational facilities. Each residential unit is designed as a separate 'house in the sky', linked by bridges to the lift core and staircases. The units have no adjoining party walls and the maximum possible external wall area for good cross ventilation, heat loss and natural lighting. All the bridges, lift lobbies and staircases are naturally ventilated; the building is not air-conditioned.

Structurally, the building has shear walls and a patented precast panel system (MBf Panel System).

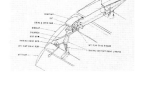

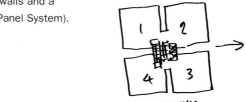

6 CONVENTIONAL COMPACT PLANNING DARK & DINGY LIFT LOBBY, POOR CROSS-VENTILATION

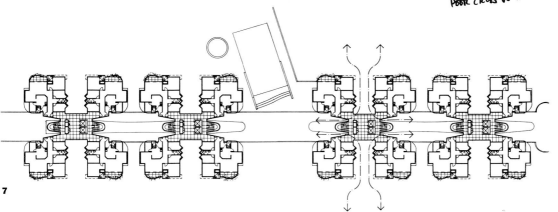

7

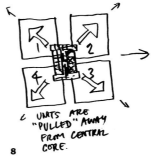

8 UNITS ARE "PULLED" AWAY FROM CENTRAL CORE.

1 Site plan
2 Concept sketch showing cross ventilation
3 Sunpath diagram
4 Section
5 Ground floor plan
6 Concept sketch: conventional central-core plan
7 Typical floor plan: 1st–11th floors
8 Concept sketch showing units pulled away from central core
8 Elevation

9

EuroTower

Location:
Europe

Size:
Restaurant and viewing
platform: 200 m²;
height: 100 m

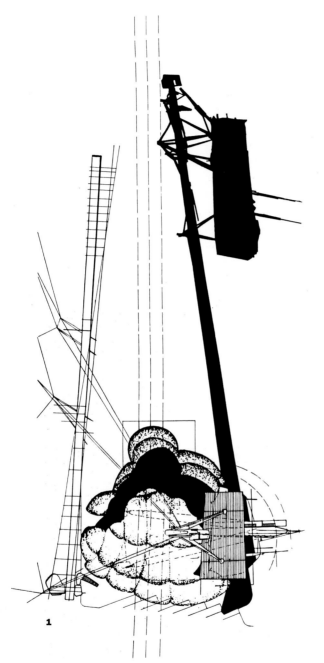

1

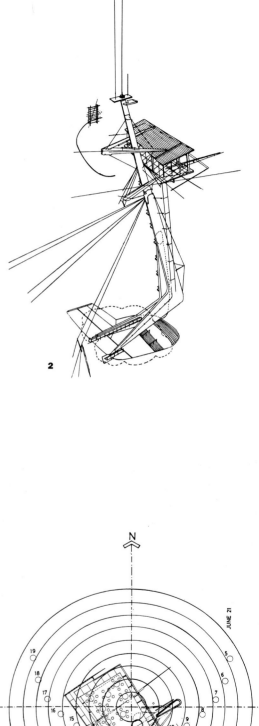

2

3

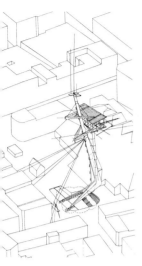

The structure is intended to create an urban icon to take a contemporary European city into the 21st century by building on the its historic past.

The brief set out certain constraints on the location of the vertical element. The manipulation of the tower, while complying with these constraints, creates a variable enclosure to be used as a public meeting space and to provide access to the underground station. The main structural element of the tower, the mast, cantilevers to create a sense of directional motion, thus emphasizing the progressive nature of the city. It also frees the ground area to be used as a public space. There is minimal interference to existing services running through the site.

A secondary cantilevered structure is suspended from the mast to complete the tower, Within this is a viewing platform and restaurant fronted by a sliding solar shield.

The public enclosure, relating to the environmental design considerations of the location, adapts to the bioclimatic variations of the inside/outside and day/night relationships, the seasonal variations, and solar orientation. These climate and site-specific factors are addressed by the design of various kinetic solar-screening devices and heat-retention wraps.

EUROTOWER

5

1 Site plan
2 Axonometric view (drawn by James Philips)
3 Sunpath diagram
4 Contextual view
5 Model: viewing platform and restaurant
6 Model: general view

6

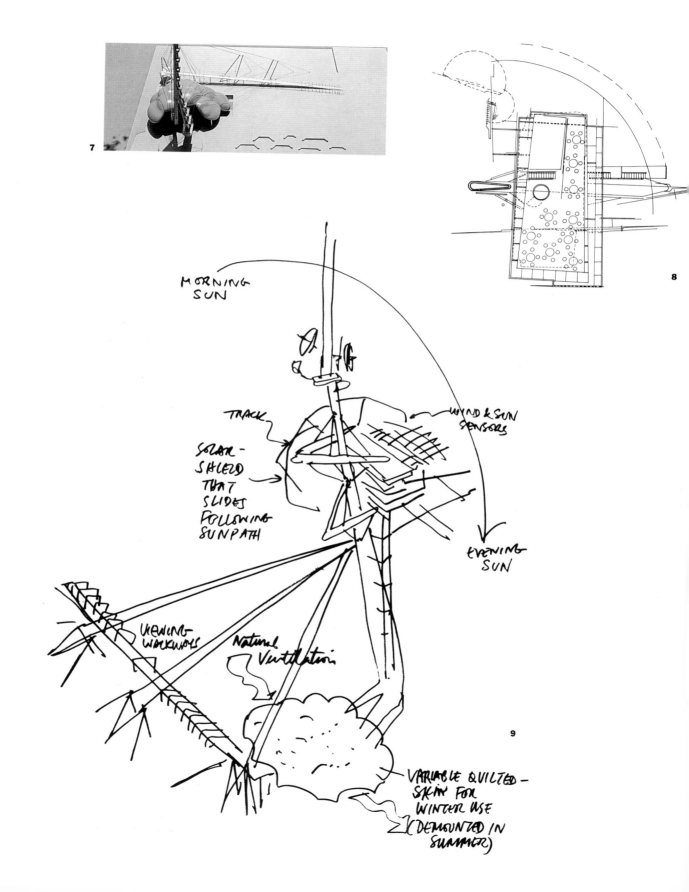

7

8

MORNING SUN

TRACK

SOLAR-SHIELD THAT SLIDES FOLLOWING SUNPATH

WIND & SUN SENSORS

EVENING SUN

VIEWING WALKWAYS

Natural Ventilation

9

VARIABLE QUILTED-SKIN FOR WINTER USE (DEMOUNTED IN SUMMER)

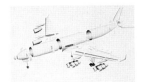

11

7 Model: detail of demountable ground-level enclosure
8 Plan: viewing platform
9 Concept sketch
10 Model
11 Model

Tokyo–Nara Tower

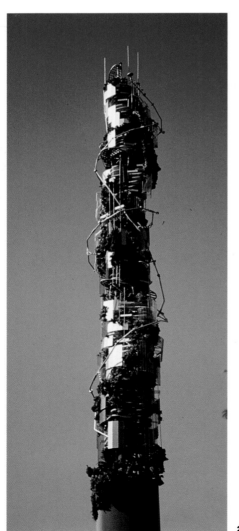

Location
somewhere between Tokyo
and Nara, Japan

Client
Nara Municipal Office

Size
4,828,160 m² gross
(4,603,603 m² net);
80 storeys

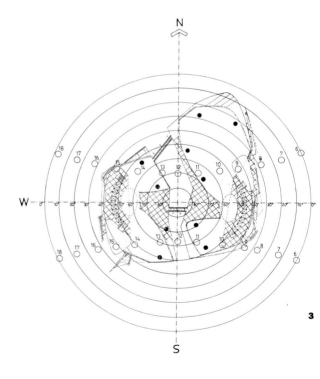

This is a project prepared for a site between Tokyo and Nara.

The ideas behind its conception can be summarized as:
• Vertical landscaping, spiralling around, through, and inside the built form. The verdant foliage cools the building; the fringing of floors and atrial spaces allows careful planting to control air movements within the structure; the mass of planting relative to the built structure means that the biosystems can act symbiotically with mechanical systems to provide a balanced environment.
• Specialized mechanical devices and cherry pickers on tracks to maintain the vertical landscaping as well as the external fixtures, glazing and cladding panels. These are constructed in the form of multi-purpose robot arms on moveable trellises.
• The radial/spiral movement of floor planes creates a particular built form that allows the floors to shade themselves as they spiral up. The displaced pattern exploits the benefits of hanging gardens, inter-floor bracing and ventilation systems and provides a constantly changing atrial space, articulated by terraces, internal courts and private gardens.
• Regularly spaced skycourt oases provide inhabitants with environmentally sound breaks in the built structure. These green parks, suspended high above the city, act as the tower's lungs.
• Atrial spaces, winding within the the tower, are the arterial routes by which floors interact. The atrial network, bridged by walkways and flanked by stairwells, constitutes a microcosm of activity, within the tower (while open to the environment) and insulated from the city.
• Lift and service cores are laid along the east–west axis. The cooler façades on the north–south axis are left open by clear glazing and atrial voids.
• The sides of the building along the east–west axis are more solidly glazed, with cast and perforated metal cladding, than those on the north–south axis which have open louvres, tiered sun shades and clear glazing.

PLECTRUM SHAPED FLOOR PLATES ROTATED ALTERNATE FLOOR

4

Roof-top garden

Intermediate gardens

STEPPED TERRACES & PLANTERS   4

(GARDENS & SKY-COURTS)

1 Location plan
2 Model
3 Sunpath diagram
4 Concept sketches: eccentric floorplates and stepped terraces
5 Detail of model

5

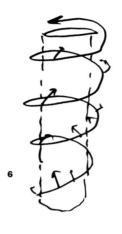

SERVICE
TRACK
THAT
SPIRALS
UP THE
BUILDING
WITH
MOBILE
"CHERRY-
PICKERS"

6

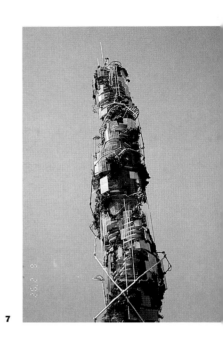

7

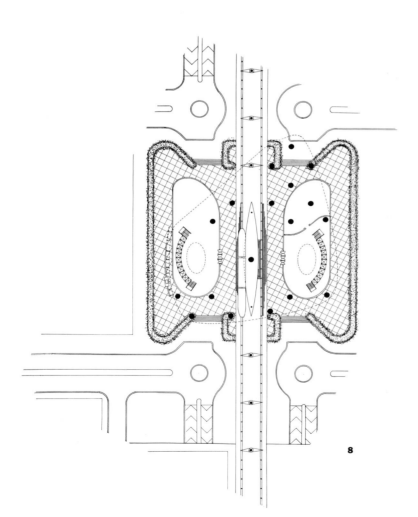

8

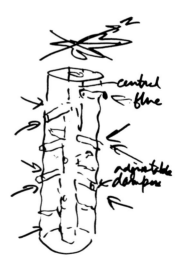

6

WIND FLUES
TO BRING
WIND TO
INNER PARTS
OF THE
BUILDING.
WITH
ADJUSTABLE
DAMPERS

6

ROTATING
MOVEABLE
SUN-SHADES
& WIND-SHIELDS

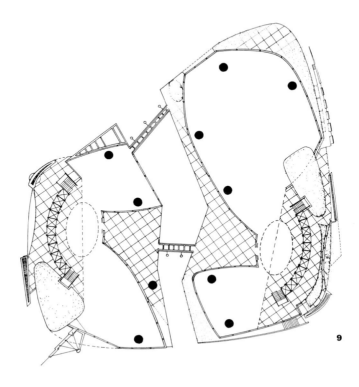

9

11

10

6 Concept sketches: spiral
service track; flues
bringing wind to the inner
parts of the building;
sun shading

7 Model

8 Ground floor plan

9 Typical floor plan

10 Sketch: mobile 'cherry
picker' (drawn by Paul
Matthews)

11 Model

China Tower No. 1
1994–

1

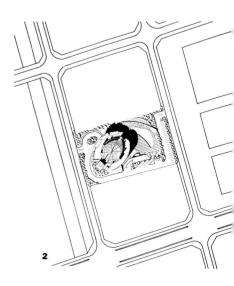

2

Location
Haikou, Hainan, People's
Republic of China

Client
Shi-Hua

Size
42,905 m² gross; 35 storeys

Plot ratio
1:4.7

3

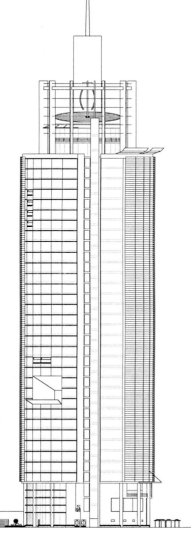

N

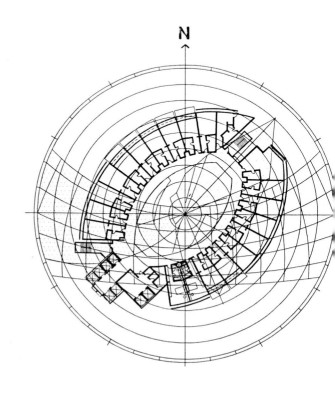

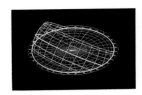

This hotel tower's design is part of a continuing investigation of the use of wind as an ambient bioclimatic component. It explores the use of the predominant north-easterly and south-easterly winds.

In the middle of the tower (oval in plan) is an atrium punctuated on both sides by cut-out skycourts with sun scoops reflecting daylight into the atrium. The tower's aerodynamic shape is oriented so that the tip of the oval faces towards the prevailing wind which is then ducted through ceiling plenums to ventilate the inner parts of the building. The wind is controlled by adjustable louvres that are externally sensor-controlled and monitored. A wind-powered generator is situated at the top of the building; the electricity produced is stored in batteries and provides water heating, lighting for the main and escape stairs, and emergency lighting.

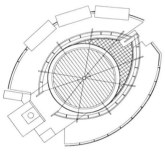

7

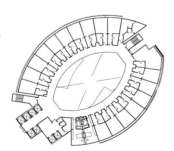

9

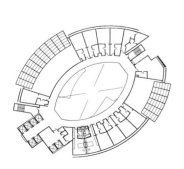

1 Computer model: bird's-eye view
2 Site plan
3 North elevation
4 Sunpath diagram
5 Model
6 Plan: roof level
7 Typical floor plan
8 Plan: level 11
9 Model

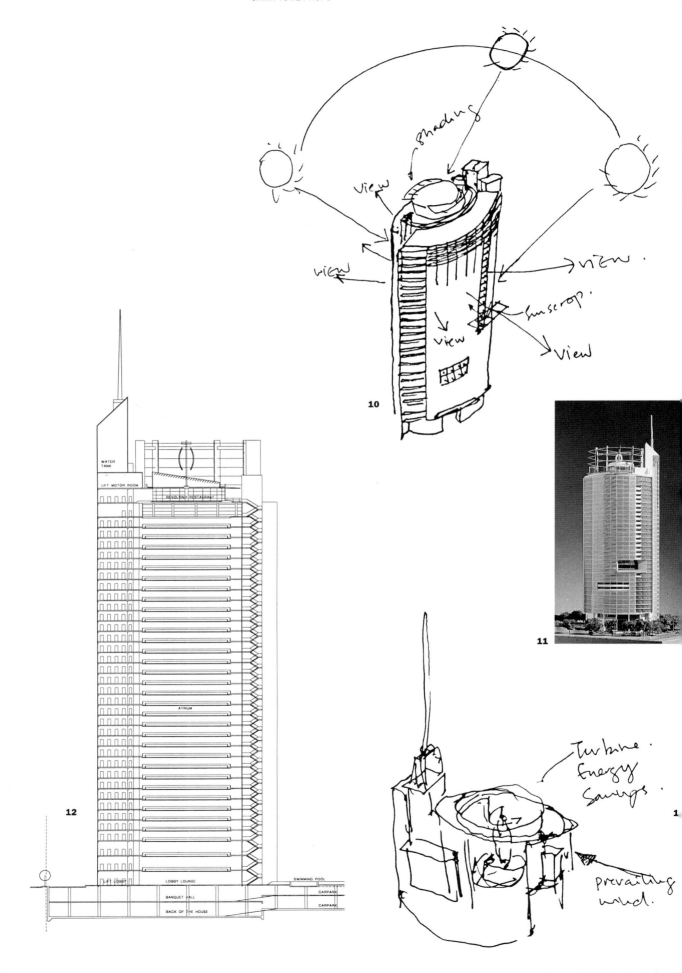

10

11

12

WATER TANK

LIFT MOTOR ROOM

REVOLVING RESTAURANT

ATRIUM

LIFT LOBBY
LOBBY LOUNGE
SWIMMING POOL
BANQUET HALL
CARPARK
BACK OF THE HOUSE
CARPARK

C H I N A T O W E R N O. 1

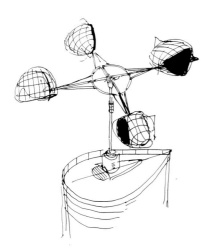

15

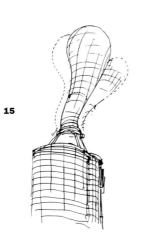

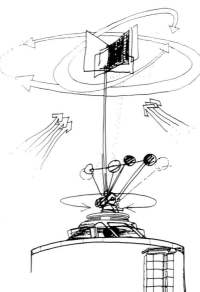

10 Concept sketch: shading and views (drawn by Ng En Loong)

11 Model

12 Section through atrium

13 Concept sketch: wind turbine

14 Plan view of model

15 Sketches: wind turbines (drawn by Battle McCarthy)

China Tower No. 2
1994–

1

Location
Haikou, Hainan, People's
Republic of China

Client
Shi-Hua

Size
Tower 1: 24,814 m² gross;
Tower 2: 22,660 m² gross;
36 storeys

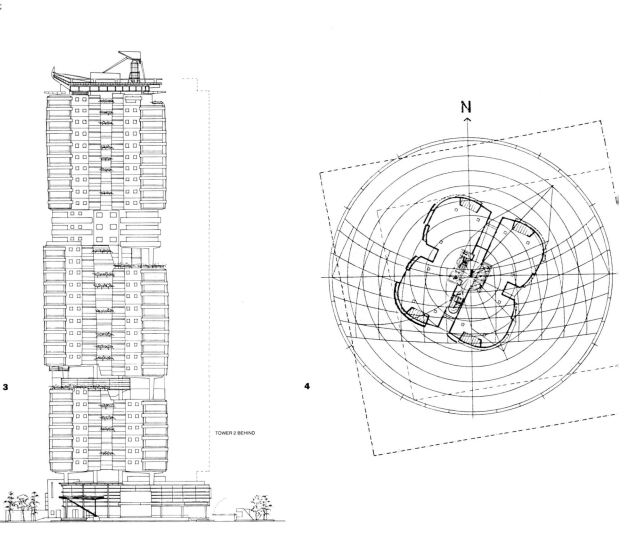

2

3

TOWER 2 BEHIND

4

N

Two up-market apartment towers facing the sea. Most floors have four apartment units; others have three with the remaining space used as skycourts and communal spaces in the sky. All the apartments have external walls on three sides and large balconies, with moveable typhoon shutters, facing the sea. Lift lobbies and staircases are naturally ventilated and the top floor houses penthouse swimming pools, sun deck and wind-powered generators.

6

1 Computer model
2 Location plan
3 North-east elevation
4 Sunpath diagram
5 Model
6 Section

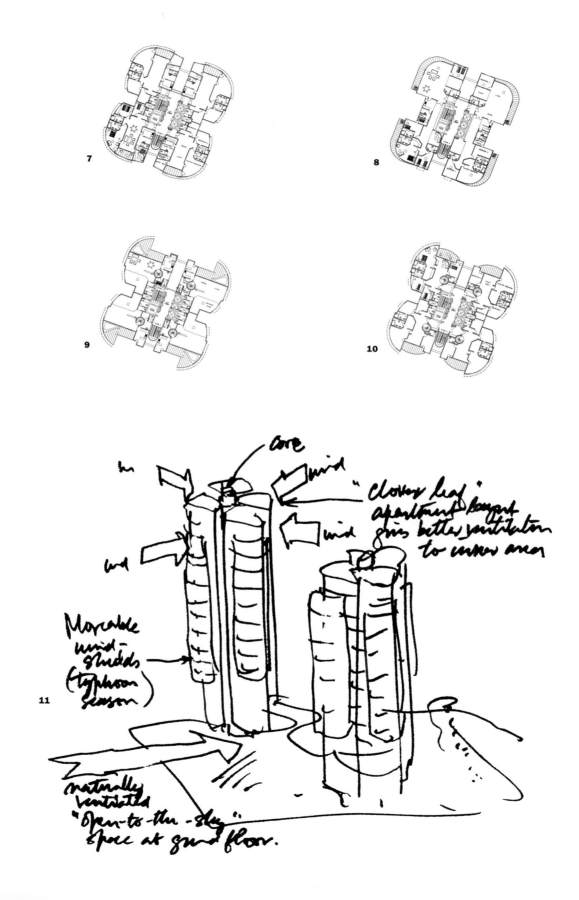

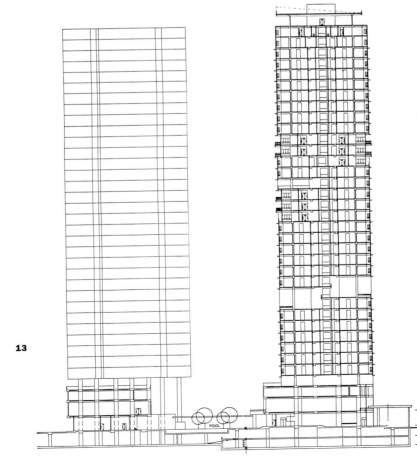

13

7 Typical floor plan: option A
8 Typical floor plan: option B
9 Typical upper floor plan:
option A
10 Typical upper floor plan:
option B
11 Concept sketch: wind
shielding and ventilation
12 Model: plan view
13 Section

China Tower No. 3
1993–

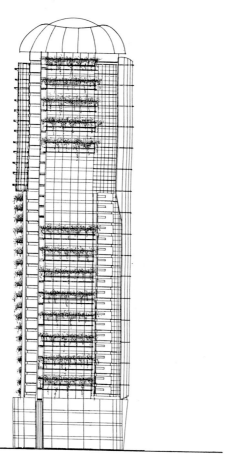

1

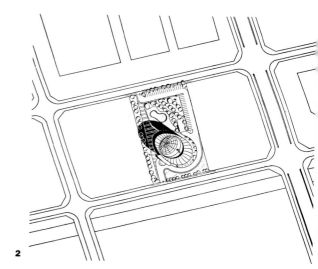

2

Location
Haikou, Hainan, People's
Republic of China

Client
Shi-Hua

Size
Tower 1: 40,650 m² gross;
36 storeys

Plot ratio
1:5.8

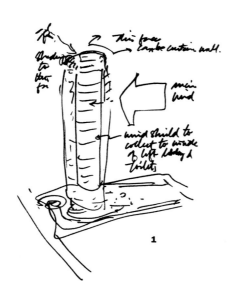

3

SOUTH ELEVATION

N

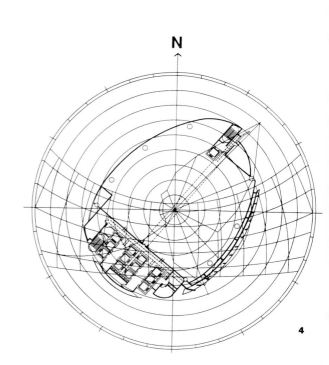

4

This office tower has an elliptical floorplate orientated to receive wind which is then channelled into the building for ventilation. A number of diverse wind-collection devices are proposed. One system is used to ventilate naturally the public lift lobbies, stairs and toilets. Another is adopted for the useable office areas.

The external wall design is solar responsive, using the principle of decreasing density of sun shading. The north- and south-facing facets of the wall are unshaded. At the top of the building is a revolving restaurant. This is combined with a large wind scoop.

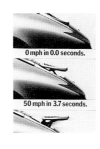

0 mph in 0.0 seconds.

50 mph in 3.7 seconds.

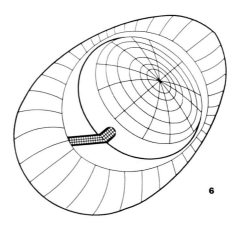

6

7

1 Concept sketch: wind shielding and sun shading (drawn by Battle McCarthy)
2 Location plan
3 Elevation
4 Sunpath diagram
5 Model
6 Elliptical roof plan
7 Model

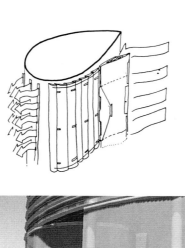

8

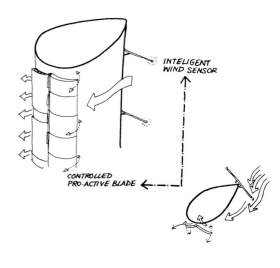

INTELIGENT
WIND SENSOR

CONTROLLED
PRO·ACTIVE BLADE

9

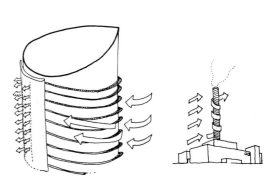

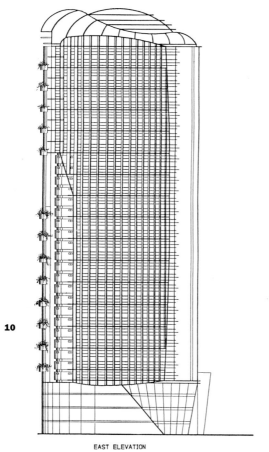

10

EAST ELEVATION

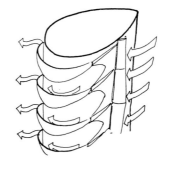

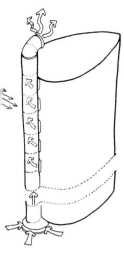

11

8 Study sketches: wind collection and control devices

9 Model: detail of entrance

10 Elevation

11 Bird's-eye view of model

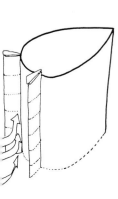

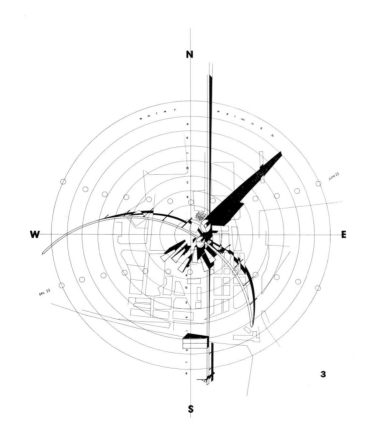

1

Location
Johor Basu, Johor

Client
MPJB

Size
60 storeys

Plot ratio
more than 1:10

3

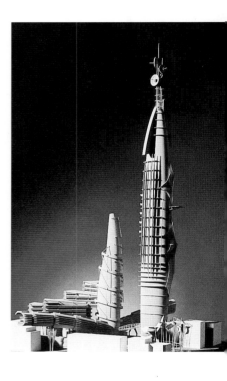

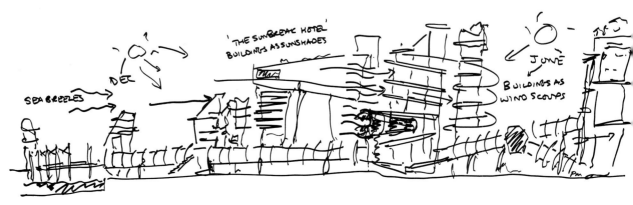

The bioclimatic city reacts like the human body to changes in its environment. As the body maintains its organic stability, for example by cooling via its extremities and by its homeostatic systems, so can the tropical city employ cooling layers and use the principles of homeostasis to maintain levels of comfort.

In the bioclimatic city, the role of the architect is to identify and design new structures, devices and spaces to protect and enhance climatically the local urban environment, meeting criteria to improve existing layers of bioclimatic control. Thus additional layers are assigned a co-ordinated form according to the city's needs as it grows and changes, allowing a three-dimensional superimposition and layering to take place over existing layers, cooling and shading the living organism of the city.

Within the many diverse spaces of the city, people are cooled while some of the structures themselves act as sun-shading devices to existing pedestrian routes. These routes intersect at specific urban spaces designed to act as places for interaction, protected by small canopy-like structures which jostle in the wind that is channelled through structures acting as wind scoops, providing constant fresh air and cooling breezes. These same buildings also shade the city as a homeostatic organism – buildings themselves act as giant sun shades. Vegetation on roofs, walls and plazas provides further recreation areas, gardens in the sky, while cooling the city's structures.

The idea of the city as a wind-channeling and cooling apparatus further serves all pedestrian areas. Moving air is channelled into these areas and passes through small water jets placed along the route, thus lowering the air temperature dramatically. The cooled air falls, creating a wave of cold air dropping to the lower layers of the bioclimatic city.

Commercial developments harness the cooling sea breezes and transform wind to energy for portions of the pedestrian travelators. Internally, the city's new telecommunications tower uses the wind to cool the enclosed spaces below using wind-wing walls for directing natural ventilation. The façades of the commercial developments would also selectively force the ambient wind to flow towards the lower layers and spaces of the garden city.

JB
2005

6

1 Model: interface with street
2 Model
3 Sunpath diagram
4 Study sketches (drawn by Paul Matthews/Rachel Atthis)
5 Model: bird's-eye view
6 Model: buildings sheltering the street

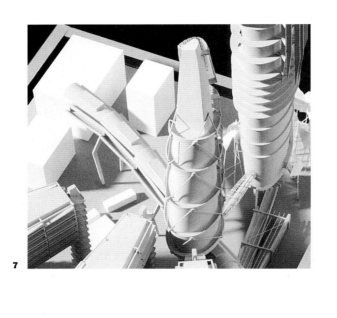

7

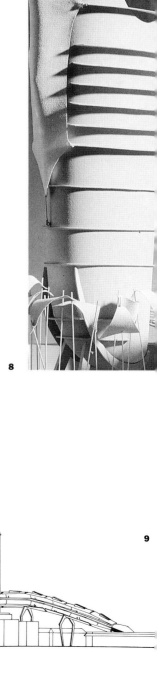

8

9

11

J
B
2
0
0
5

7 Model: detail of
small tower
8 Model
9 East–west section
10 North–south
section
11 Model

Appendix:
Climate & Design

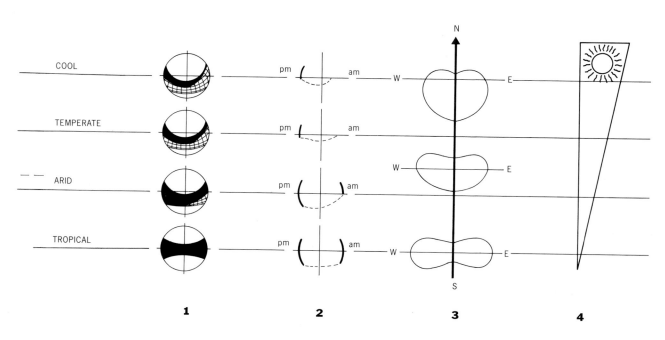

1   2   3   4

1   SOLAR PATHS REQUIRING SHADE

Analyzing the sunpath diagram for each zone, the shaded areas represent the periods of overheating, related to undesirable solar gain. In the lower latitudes there is total overheating, whereas in the higher latitudes overheating only occurs during the summer months.

2   SUNSHADE ANALYSIS (VERTICAL AND HORIZONTAL)

The diagrams show the optimum location of vertical sun shading, shielding the building from low sun angles in the morning and evening, and horizontal sun shading blocking the high midday sun. Tropical regions need both vertical and horizontal shading throughout the year. In higher latitudes, horizontal and vertical shading is only needed during the summer on the south-facing sides of buildings.

3   INSOLATION

The sunpath becomes more southerly as we move north, changing from a 'bow-tie' pattern near the equator to a heart-shape pattern in the temperate zones.

4   SUN REQUIREMENT DURING WINTER

There are obviously seasonal variations near the equator. Solar heating becomes more important than in the upper latitudes.

Climatic Zones

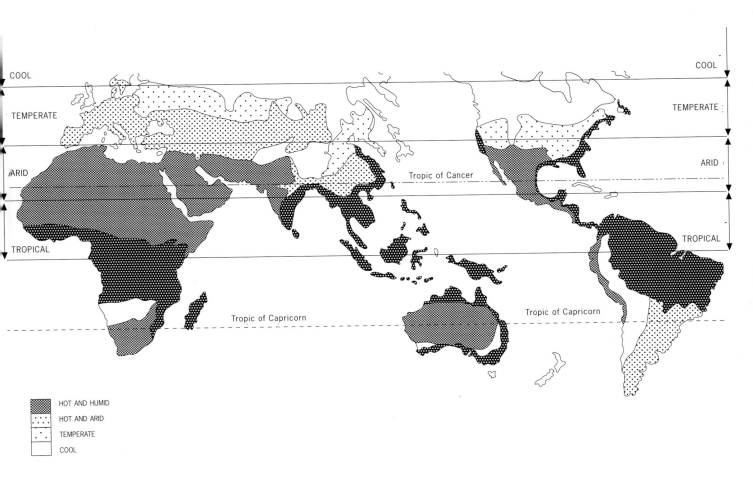

COOL

TEMPERATE

ARID

TROPICAL

Tropic of Cancer

Tropic of Capricorn

Tropic of Capricorn

COOL

TEMPERATE

ARID

TROPICAL

HOT AND HUMID
HOT AND ARID
TEMPERATE
COOL

The four major climatic zones are: tropical; arid; temperate; cool. These can be analyzed in terms of architectural response to varying climatic conditions. Examining the unique conditions obtaining in each major climatic zone, a programme of research, design and development (RD&D) was initiated to develop the bioclimatic tall-building type. The method involves first analyzing each zone's climate characteristics, then their influences on built form, followed by more detailed research into the use of the external wall as an interactive filter. The traditional built forms' characteristics are also examined.

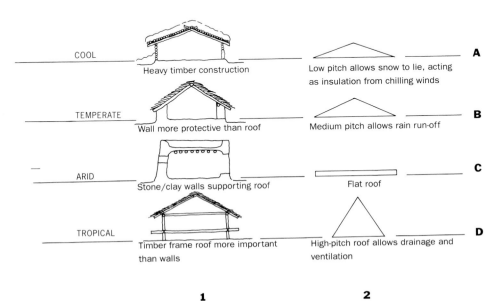

COOL — Heavy timber construction — A — Low pitch allows snow to lie, acting as insulation from chilling winds

TEMPERATE — Wall more protective than roof — B — Medium pitch allows rain run-off

ARID — Stone/clay walls supporting roof — C — Flat roof

TROPICAL — Timber frame roof more important than walls — D — High-pitch roof allows drainage and ventilation

1   **2**

1   TRADITIONAL REGIONAL DWELLING TYPES

Analyzing the traditional low-rise dwelling type in each climatic zone, the nature of the relationship between climate , built form and materials can be further understood.

2   TYPICAL OCCURENCE OF INDIGENOUS ROOF TYPES

Analyzing the roof type of traditional dwellings, the climate can be further understood for the low-rise building type.

A – Increase heat production
– Increase radiation absorption
– Decrease radiation heat loss
– Reduce conduction and evaporation loss

C – Increase heat production
– Reduce and promote loss of radiation
– Reduce conduction gain
– Promote evaporation

B – A balance should be established by reducing or promoting on a seasonal basis the heat production, radiation and convection effects

D – Reduce heat production
– Reduce radiation gain
– Promote evaporation loss

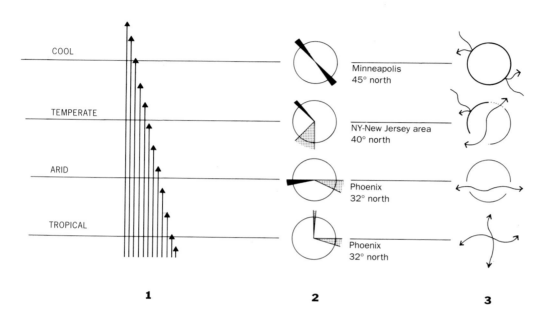

COOL

TEMPERATE

ARID

TROPICAL

Minneapolis
45° north

NY-New Jersey area
40° north

Phoenix
32° north

Phoenix
32° north

1   **2**   **3**

1   REQUIREMENTS FOR CROSS VENTILATION

Cross ventilation is far more important in the tropics than in temperate zones.

▨   DESIRED WIND DIRECTION
■   UNDESIRED WIND DIRECTION

2   WIND DIRECTION

Desired and undesired winds in each of the climatic zones depend largely on local conditions. Any breeze in the lower latitudes (tropical and arid climates) is beneficial whereas in higher latitudes most wind is detrimental.

3   CROSS-VENTILATION ANALYSIS

The theoretical strategy for blocking or inducing wind flow into a building is based on local prevailing wind conditions. Generally, for the tropical zone as much ventilation as possible is desired. For the arid zone cross ventilation is required, but care has to be taken to filter out high-velocity winds.

    In the temperate zone, cross ventilation and shielding are both necessary.

    In the cool region, the building should be protected from cold, high-velocity winds, although cross ventilation is still required.

Climatic Characteristics

Climatic zones are analyzed acording to a specific climatic characteristic, allowing visual comparisons of the results to be made.

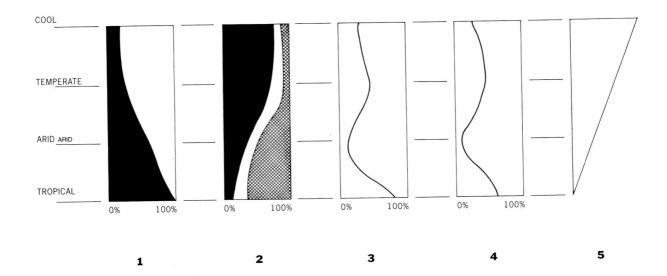

1 **ANNUAL % OF REQUIRED SOLAR SHADING AND SOLAR HEATING**
Beginning at the Equator and moving north, the need for solar heating increases while the need for solar shading diminishes.

- ▬ SOLAR SHADING
- ▭ SOLAR HEATING

2 **ANNUAL % OF REQUIRED WIND SCREENING**
The shaded (black) area represents the percentage of wind screening required for comfort throughout the year.

The hatched area represents the percentage of breezes needed for comfortable conditions.

The unshaded area represents the percentage of the year when comfortable conditions are achieved naturally, without any need for wind screening or additional breezes.

It can be seen that cooling by breezes is necessary in the lower latitudes for most of the year while at higher latitudes nearly all wind has to be screened. Each zone has a small percentage of the year which is comfortable.

- ▬ WIND SCREENING
- ▭ COMFORT
- ▦ BREEZES

3 **ANNUAL AVERAGE LEVEL OF RELATIVE HUMIDITY**
The curve represents the annual average level of relative humidity in the four climatic zones. In the arid zone, the low level of humidity can be beneficial for evaporative cooling. In the tropical zone the high level of humidity can be very uncomfortable.

4 **ANNUAL AVERAGE LEVEL OF RAINFALL**
The curve represents the annual average level of rainfall in the four climatic zones. Rainfall level can be seen to have a direct relationship with humidity levels.

5 **ANNUAL SEASONAL VARIATIONS**
The distance of the angled line from the vertical represents the annual seasonal variations in the four climatic zones.

Higher latitudes, the cold and temperate zones, have pronounced seasonal variations. The lower latitudes have constant climates throughout the year.

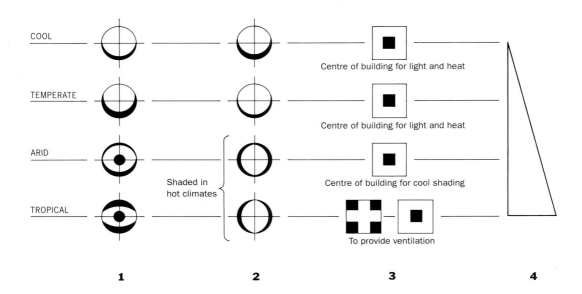

Centre of building for light and heat

Centre of building for light and heat

Centre of building for cool shading

To provide ventilation

COOL

TEMPERATE

ARID

Shaded in
hot climates

TROPICAL

1   2   3   4

1 ZONING FOR TRANSITIONAL SPACES

The black areas represent the traditional spaces used for lobbies,
stairs, utility spaces, circulation, balconies and any other areas
where movement takes place. These areas do not require total
climatic control and natural ventilation is sufficient.

For the tropical and arid zones, the transitional spaces are located
on the north and south sides of the building where the sun's
penetration is not as great. An atrium can also be used as a
transitional shaded space.

In the temperate and cool zones the transitional spaces should be
located on the south side of the building to maximize solar gain.

3 USE OF ATRIUM SPACE

The diagrams show the optimum position for atrium spaces in each
building form in each of the climatic zones.

In the tropical zone the atrium should be located so as to provide
ventilation within the built form.

In the arid zone the atrium should be located at the centre of the
building for cooling and shading purposes.

For the cool and temperate zones the atrium should be at the
centre of the building form for heat and light.

2 ZONING FOR SOLAR GAIN

The black areas are spaces that can be used for solar heat gain.
They follow the varying path of the sun in each of the climatic zones:
in the tropical and arid zones the east and west sides; in the
temperate and cool zones the south side.

**4 POTENTIAL OF ROOF/GROUND PLANE AS USEABLE EXTERIOR
SPACE**

The distance of the angled line from the vertical represents the
potential of each zone's roof and ground planes to be used as
exterior space.

In tropical and arid climates there is a high potential to make use
of all external spaces, whereas moving towards the northern
latitudes the external spaces have to be covered to be used.

Influences on Built Form

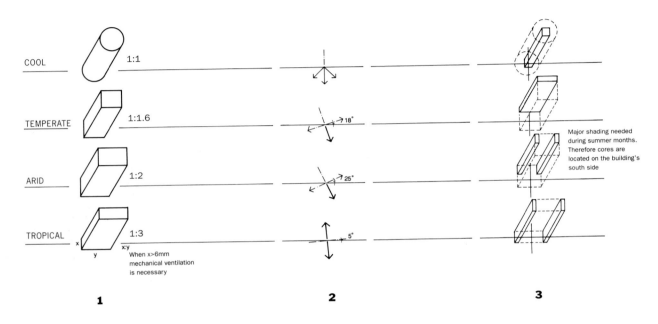

COOL   1:1

TEMPERATE   1:1.6   18°

ARID   1:2   25°

TROPICAL   x   x:y   1:3   5°

y

When x>6mm mechanical ventilation is necessary

Major shading needed during summer months. Therefore cores are located on the building's south side

1   **2**   **3**

1 FORM

The diagrams show the optimum building form for each climatic zone. Research has shown that the preferred length of the sides of the building, where the sides are of length x:y, are:

- tropical zone   1:3
- arid zone   1:2
- temperate zone   1:1.6
- cool zone   1:1

Analysis of these ratios shows that an elongated form to minimize east and west exposure is needed at the lower latitudes. This form slowly transforms to a ratio of 1:1 (cylindrical) at the higher latitudes. This is a direct response to the varying solar angles in the various latitudes.

2 ORIENTATION

Orientation as well as directional emphasis changes with latitude in response to solar angles.

Zone	Building's main orientations	Directional emphasis
Tropical	on an axis 5° north of east	north–south
Arid	on an axis 25° north of east	south–east
Temperate	on an axis 18° north of east	south–south-east
Cool	on an axis facing south	facing south

3 VERTICAL CORES AND STRUCTURE

The arrangement of primary mass can be used as a factor in bioclimatic design as its position can help to shade or retain heat within the building form.

For the tropical zone, the cores are located on the east and west sides of the building form, so as to help shade the building from the low angles of the sun during the major part of the day.

In the arid zone, the cores should also be located on the east and west sides, but with major shading only needed during the summer. Therefore, the cores are located on the east and west sides, but primarily on the south side.

The arrangement of the primary mass in the temperate zone is on the north face, so as to leave the south face available for solar heat gain during the winter.

The cool zone requires the maximum perimeter of the building to be open to the sun for heat penetration. Therefore the primary mass is placed in the centre of the building so as not to block out the sun's rays and to retain heat within the building.

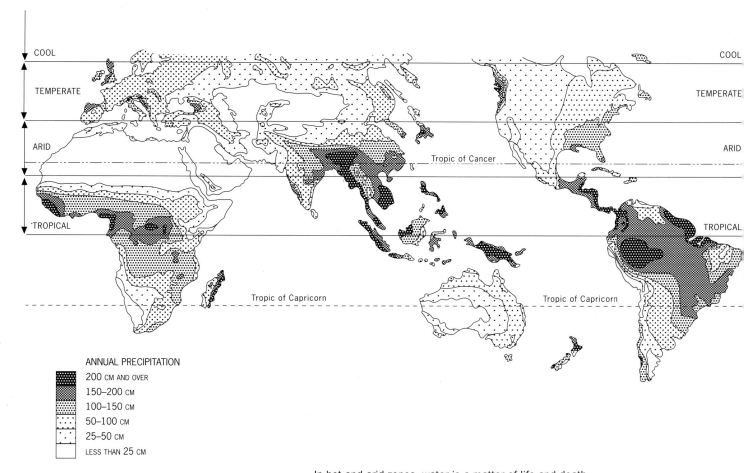

COOL

TEMPERATE

ARID

TROPICAL

Tropic of Cancer

Tropic of Capricorn

Tropic of Capricorn

COOL

TEMPERATE

ARID

TROPICAL

ANNUAL PRECIPITATION

200 CM AND OVER

150–200 CM

100–150 CM

50–100 CM

25–50 CM

LESS THAN 25 CM

In hot and arid zones, water is a matter of life and death.
The annual rainfall for the world as a whole is 8.6cm,
compared to less than 2.5cm in the hot and arid zones.
Added to this is the greater variability of precipitation in
these regions, accompanied by high evaporation rates.

Acknowledgements

T R Hamzah & Yeang Sdn Bhd
Staff 1991–1993
Adrian Hazizi Hashim
Ahmad Kamil Mustapha
Ahmad Mirza Hamzah
Ahmad Nazri Jaafar
Ang Chee Cheong
Ania Stolinska
Asmadi bin Jusoh
Azahari Muhammad, Vedo
Azhar Hj Sidek
Azmin Abdullah
Brian Rogers
Chan Tai Ngok
Charles Peh
Chew Loo See
Chin Weng Yin, Thomas
Ching Sow Lin, Irene
Chong Kim Yong
Chong Soon Onn
Chong Voon Wee
Chow Kin Hoong
Chow Kok Cheong
Chua Caik Leng
Don Ismail Allan
Edward Jackson
Eilir W Sheryn
Emmy Ying-Li Lim
Erica Gilbert
Ernest Teh
Fadzillah Mohd Fadzil
Foo Chong Yee
Frederieke van Ellen
Fu Kam Sang
Gillian Wan
Haslina Ali
Haslina Yaakob
Hazlinda Hashim
Heng Jee Seng
Indrani E Vanniasingham
Ismail Awab
James Allan Finnie
James Chin Wei Mean
James Chua
James Ng
James Phillips
Jay Low
Kamariah
Kayate bte Sukadis
L Selvasubramaniam
Lam Chow Yuen
Laurence Liauw
Laurent Lim
Lim Oh Seng
Lim Pay Chye
Lim Piek Boon
Loh Mun Chee
Lucille Lim
Mah Lek

Mak Fook Chin
Mak Wei Mun
Margaret Ng
Mariani Abdullah
Mark Gurney
Mary Lui
Megat Rozlan Abd Rahman
Megat Sharizal
MichaelSimmons
Mohd Sabri
Mohd Zolzamzuri Hassan
Nadarajan a/l Nadesan
Ng Boon Teck
Ng En-Loong
Ng Kim Teh
Ng See Leng, Derick
Ng Wai Tuck
Ng Yu Thian
Ngooi Voon Fong
Noor Aliyah Md Ali
Noraini Ahmad
Norasmah Mohd Hashim
Normala Hj Ariffin
Normala Ismail
Norziana Yusoff
Ong Boon Hing
Ooi Poh Lye
Paul Matthews
Peter Ho
Puvan Selvanathan
Quaik Lian See
Rachel Atthis
Rahimah Mohd Lasim
Raja Hidzir bin Raja Khalid
Razidah bte Mohd Sharif
Rohailan Mohammad
Roslan Mohamed Amin
Ruby Loo
Rukiyah Samsuddin
Sacha Ramlan Noordin
Sarangapany a/l Muniandy
Seow Ji Nee
Sew Aileen
Shahrina Intan
Shanmuganathan a/l Perumal
Sharifah Alhabshi
Sneha Anne Mathews
Sow Sun Fong
Srazali Aripin
Suhaimi
Suriati Hassan
Suriyani bt Mohd Tahir
Tan Bee Woan
Tan Beng Kay
Tan Kim Tho, Patricia
Tay Lee Lee
Tommy Phuah
Too Ka Hoe
Victor Low Chun Pang

Voon Quek Wah
William Jude
Wong Choon Heng
Wong Tung Ken
Woo Yiw Po
Yap Lip Pien
Yap Siat Lin
Yap Yow Kong
Yeoh Gim Seong
Yew Ai Choo
Yip Phaik Yoon
Yue Yoon Wa, Janet
Yusmanisa Yusoff
Yusoff Zainal Abidin
Zakiah bt Hj Abdullah
Zurinah bt Hussein

Drawings
Raymond Soh
Srazali Aripin
Yeoh Gim Seong
Noraini bte Ahmad
Adrin Hazizi Hashim
Mariani Abdullah
Derick Ng See Leng
Emmy Ying-Li Lim
Alex Cheong
Peter Ho

Sketches
Paul Matthews
Rachel Atthis
James Phillips
Tan Kwee Yen
Battle McCarthy
Ken Yeang

Photography
K L Ng
Albert Lim
Trends Publishing (Roep
Hopman)
Ken Yeang

Models
J M Kiang (J M Kiang Modeller)
Lim Swee Eng (Technibuilt)
Mohd Nor Abdullah (Excell
Matrix)

**Bioclimatic Diagrams and
Research**
Ania Stolinska
Brian Rogers (Luce Scholar,
Luce Foundation)
Battle McCarthy
Professor John Frazer and
students (Unit 11: 1992, AA
School)
Students under Professor
Wayne Attoe (Louisiana State
University, 1991)
Students under Ho Pak Toe
(Department of Architecture,
National University of
Singapore, 1989)
Students under Professor Eric
Lye (Department of
Architecture, University of Hong
Kong, 1990)
Dr Phil Jones (Department of
Architecture, University of
Cardiff, 1993)

Guidance and Review
Tengku Robert Hamzah (T R
Hamzah & Yeang Sdn Bhd)
Professor Alan Balfour
(Chairman, AA School)
Professor Ivor Richards
(University of Wales)
Rod Sheard, Lobb Partnership
(in association with T R Hamzah
& Yeang Sdn Bhd) (STC Camera
Tower)